PARAGUAY
in Pictures

VGS

Alison Behnke

Twenty-First Century Books

Contents

INTRODUCTION — 4

THE LAND — 8
► Topography. Rivers and Lakes. Climate. Flora and Fauna. Natural Resources and Environmental Challenges. Cities.

HISTORY AND GOVERNMENT — 20
► Founding of Asunción. Jesuit Settlements. Neglect from Imperial Spain. Independence and Afterward. A Different Kind of Dictator. Francisco Solano López and the War of the Triple Alliance. An Uneasy Freedom. The Chaco War. A Series of Dictators. Stroessner's Rise and Fall. Changes and Challenges. Government.

THE PEOPLE — 38
► Ethnic Groups. Daily Life. Family Ties and Women's Lives. Health. Education.

Twenty-First Century Books
A division of Lerner Publishing Group, Inc.
241 First Avenue North
Minneapolis, MN 55401 U.S.A.

Website address: www.lernerbooks.com

CULTURAL LIFE   46

► Religion. Holidays and Festivals. Language and
  Literature. Visual Arts. Music and Dance. Food.
  Sports and Recreation.

THE ECONOMY   58

► Services and Trade. Agriculture. Manufacturing
  and Industry. Transportation. Energy. Media and
  Communications. The Future.

FOR MORE INFORMATION

► Timeline   66
► Fast Facts   68
► Currency   68
► Flag   69
► National Anthem   69
► Famous People   70
► Sights to See   72
► Glossary   73
► Selected Bibliography   74
► Further Reading and Websites   76
► Index   78

Library of Congress Cataloging-in-Publication Data

Behnke, Alison.
    Paraguay in pictures / by Alison Behnke.
        p.   cm. – (Visual geography series)
    Includes bibliographical references and index.
    ISBN 978-1-57505-962-4 (lib. bdg. : alk. paper)
    1. Paraguay–Juvenile literature. I. Title.
F2668.5.B44 2010
989.2–dc22   2008038028

Manufactured in the United States of America
1 2 3 4 5 6 – BP – 15 14 13 12 11 10

INTRODUCTION

Paraguay is a small nation in South America. Landlocked, it lacks an ocean coast. Its lush and beautiful landscape offers natural beauty as well as agricultural bounty. The country consists of a well-populated region in the east and a sparsely settled wilderness in the west. Hydroelectric dams on Paraguay's many rivers convert the energy of rushing water into electric energy.

The earliest people in the land survived by hunting wild animals and gathering plants. They were the ancestors of the indigenous (native) Guarani people. No written records exist of early Guarani history or culture. But their culture and especially their language remain important to modern Paraguay.

Paraguay's history has often been harsh. A variety of factors have limited the opportunities and freedoms of Paraguay's people. In the sixteenth century, Spain made Paraguay part of its South American empire. Controlled by foreign powers, the nation was not free to determine its own path.

Paraguay declared its independence from Spain in 1811. But even following this change, the country's peoples found they were not truly free. A series of military dictators controlled the nation for more than a century and a half. One nineteenth-century leader—Francisco Solano López—led Paraguay into a disastrous war against Uruguay, Argentina, and Brazil. The conflict was called the War of the Triple Alliance. By the time it was over, fighting and disease had killed more than half the nation's people.

Other dictators ruled with an iron fist. General Alfredo Stroessner was Paraguay's dictator from 1954 until 1989. Elected—largely without opposition—to five-year terms of office eight times, Stroessner governed Paraguay longer than any of his predecessors. To help maintain his rule, Stroessner brutally crushed dissent. He also worked harder on building the nation's economy than on improving social justice.

In 1989 Andrés Rodríguez, a powerful general in the Paraguayan army, overthrew Stroessner. Four years later, Paraguay held its first

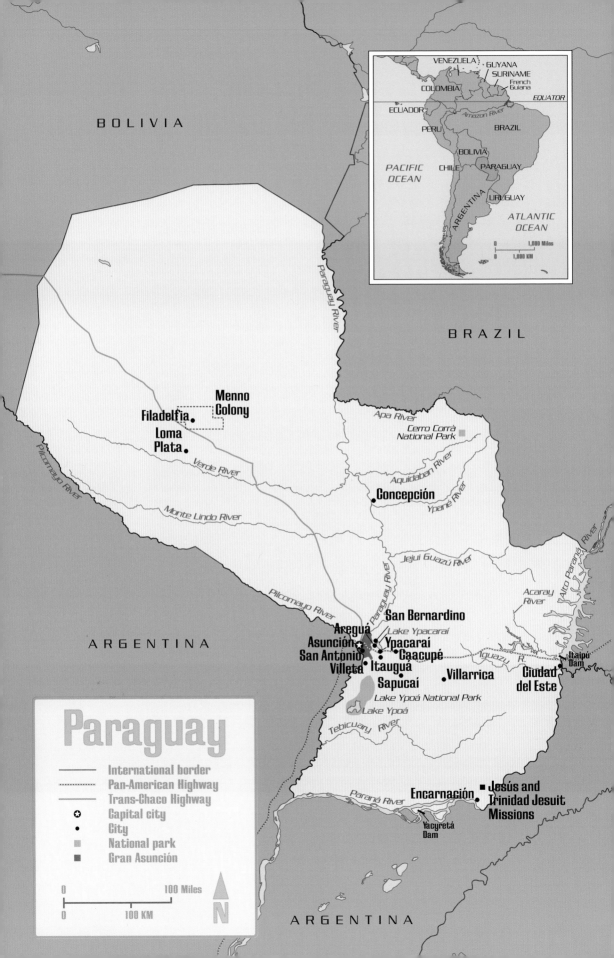

free elections. Since then peaceful and democratic elections have replaced the old ways of dictatorship. Recent presidents have struggled with problems including a faltering economy. But they have also increased Paraguayans' prosperity and freedom.

Paraguay shares its history of colonialism, dictatorship, and finally democracy with many of its South American neighbors. But the nation differs from other Spanish American countries in language and in culture. For example, most Paraguayans are bilingual, speaking not only Spanish but also Guarani—the tongue of Paraguay's indigenous inhabitants. Paraguay's music, art, and other cultural expressions also reflect both Guarani and Spanish influence.

Paraguay has overcome many of the limitations of the past. Challenges remain. For example, many of the nation's people are poor, and the gap between the rich and the poor is vast. The economy has struggled since the 1990s, and steps to improve education and health care are necessary. But Paraguayans have never let their troubles hem them in. With hard work and national pride, they are moving toward an ever brighter future.

Visit www.vgsbooks.com for links to websites with additional information about the land, history, government, people, culture, and economy of Paraguay.

THE LAND

The Republic of Paraguay is a nation in South America. The country is landlocked, meaning that it has no coastline. Argentina borders the nation on the west, the south, and the southeast. Paraguay shares much of its long eastern border with Brazil. Bolivia lies to the north. With an area of 157,048 square miles (406,752 square kilometers), Paraguay is slightly smaller than the U.S. state of California.

Topography

Paraguay consists of two main geographical regions, the Paraneña and the Gran Chaco. The Paraguay River flows from north to south between these two areas. To the river's east lies the Paraneña. This area holds part of the huge Paraná Plateau, as well as ranges of hills and valleys. One of these ranges includes Paraguay's highest point, Cerro Pero, a peak that rises 2,762 feet (842 m) above sea level. West of the river is the Gran Chaco, a massive wilderness area.

The main feature of Paraguay's Paraneña region is the Paraná

Plateau. This huge flatland extends into Paraguay from southern Brazil. In easternmost Paraguay, the plateau is a flat and grassy area. Moving westward, the plateau grows hillier and higher, eventually becoming a steep slope topped by high cliffs. Parts of this region are 1,000 to 2,000 feet (305 to 610 meters) above sea level.

West of the plateau but still within the Paraneña, two main series of hills extend into central Paraguay. One stretches toward the northern city of Concepción. The other reaches the capital, Asunción. Between these hilly ridges lie lowlands that stretch toward the Paraguay River. Some of these low areas flood annually when rivers overflow their banks.

The Paraneña holds Paraguay's most fertile land and, as a result, is home to most of the nation's people. In particular, many Paraguayans live among the highlands between Asunción and Encarnación, a city in southeastern Paraguay.

The Gran Chaco, in western Paraguay, is the nation's other main

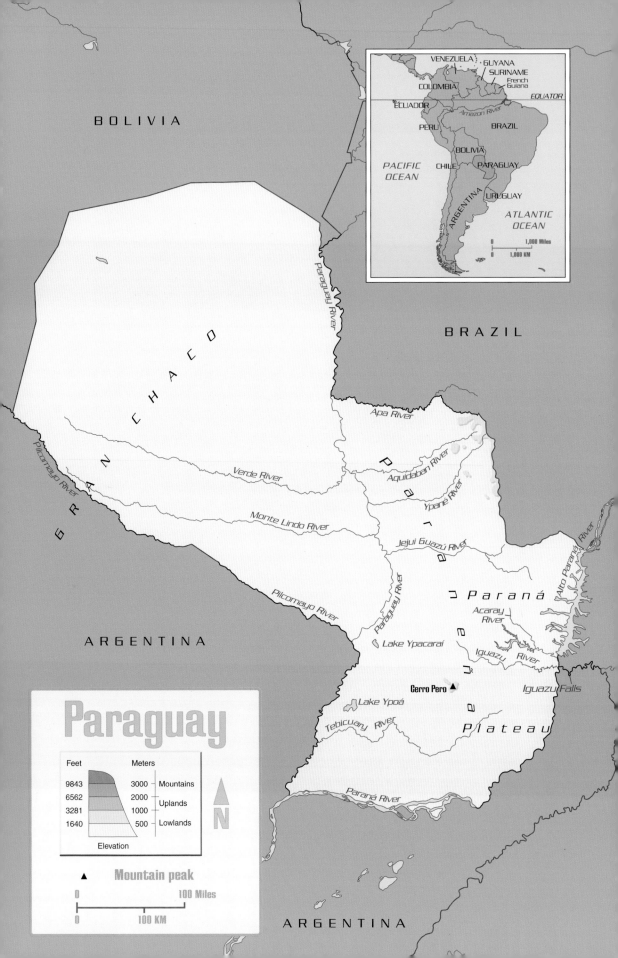

Palm trees and grasses grow on the savannas of the **Gran Chaco** in Paraguay. The Gran Chaco extends beyond Paraguay into Bolivia and Argentina.

region. Stretching from the Paraguay River to the Bolivian border, it is larger than the Paraneña. It makes up about 60 percent of Paraguay's total area. The Chaco formed thousands of years ago. At that time, flowing water deposited alluvium (silt, sand, clay, gravel, or other loose material) across the region. The resulting landform is called an alluvial plain.

In modern Paraguay, the Gran Chaco is a remote area of scrub forests and grasslands called savannas. Most of this lowland region is swampy during the rainy season and parched during the dry season. Villages and farms dot the region, with the heaviest settlement along the Paraguay River. But the region's terrain is harsh and difficult to access. As a result, the Gran Chaco has long been a sparsely inhabited wilderness. By the twenty-first century, a new road through the Chaco had begun encouraging more people to settle in the region. Nevertheless, it remains a mostly wild and little-developed area, home to less than 5 percent of the nation's inhabitants.

◉ Rivers and Lakes

Rivers are Paraguay's lifelines. Before the age of air travel, the nation's waterways were its only means of contact and communication with the world. Some of the river basins (the land that rivers drain) hold farmlands that are important for the country's survival and development. And rivers supply modern Paraguay with all the electricity that it needs. They also produce extra power, which the nation sells to its South American neighbors.

The Paraguay River is one of the most important in the nation.

The **Paraguay River** carries water to some of the country's most fertile land.

This waterway flows southward across the country after defining part of Paraguay's border with Brazil. Much of Paraguay's population lives along the banks of this river. In some places, people still wash their clothes in the river's silty waters, as Paraguayans have for centuries. Farmers divert the river's flow to irrigate their fields. Producers of meat, timber, cotton, tobacco, and other crops rely on riverboats to carry their goods to world markets. The whistling of rivercraft is a frequent sound in Paraguay. It signals the arrival and departure of people and products.

The Paraguay River flows into the Paraná River. After these rivers join, the mighty Paraná moves about 800 miles (1,287 km) into the Río de la Plata. This waterway flows between Argentina and Uruguay and finally into the Atlantic Ocean. In eastern Paraguay, the Alto Paraná River—the upper part of the Paraná River—cuts a deep trench through the Paraná Plateau. In the east and south, the Alto Paraná marks the boundary between Paraguay and Brazil and between Paraguay and northern Argentina.

Nearby, along the border between Brazil and Argentina, the Iguazu River foams over a high ledge at Iguazu. Here the river forms a great waterfall before joining the Alto Paraná. Visible from Paraguay, Iguazu Falls are much higher and larger than North America's Niagara Falls.

The Aquidaban, Ypané, and Jejui Guazú rivers are additional waterways in eastern Paraguay. Others include the Apa, which runs along part of Paraguay's border with Brazil, and the Tebicuary, which flows through the southern Paraneña. The Acaray River, near the Brazil and Argentina borders, has been the site of a hydro-electric plant since 1968.

The Gran Chaco has fewer rivers than the Paraneña. The Verde and Monte Lindo rivers flow eastward from the Gran Chaco into the Paraguay River. Also flowing from the west out of the Gran Chaco, the Pilcomayo River traces Paraguay's southwestern border with Argentina. The Pilcomayo eventually flows into the Paraguay River at Asunción.

Paraguay also holds several lakes. Ypoá Lake is located about 40 miles (64 km) south of the capital city of Asunción. The shallow Lake Ypacaraí lies about 18 miles (29 km) east of Asunción. Ypacaraì is a favorite vacation spot for many Paraguayans. Its beaches and lovely scenery attract summer visitors, and the lakeshore town of San Bernardino is a popular resort. Other small lagoons and swamps also lie scattered around Paraguay.

WHAT'S IN A NAME?

The Gran Chaco's name comes from a word in Quechua, an indigenous language in South America. The Quechua word *chaqu* means "hunting land" and probably described the Chaco's rich variety of animal life. The Paraná River's name also comes from an indigenous word, this time from the Tupi language of Brazil (a language related to Paraguay's Guarani language). The word *paraná* means "like the sea," probably referring to the wide river's expanse.

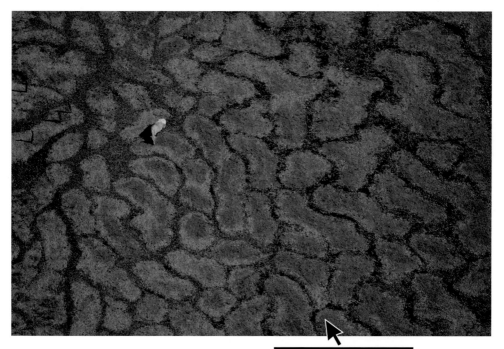

A cow grazes on the rich, swampy land of Lake Ypoá National Park.

Climate

Paraguay's climate is subtropical, with some weather conditions similar to Florida's climate. Because Paraguay is in the Southern Hemisphere (south of the equator), winter lasts from June to August, and summer is from December to March. While winter is cooler than summer, Paraguay's climate is usually warm and mild year-round.

During the winter, thermometers in Paraguay record highs of about 75°F (24°C). At night the temperatures may drop to about 55°F (13°C) or below but very rarely reach as low as freezing. Snow is rare and never falls at all in some parts of the country.

In the summer, temperatures range from lows of about 75°F (24°C) to highs of about 95°F (35°C). The average summer temperature is 83°F (28°C), but thermometers occasionally record highs of up to 110°F (43°C). The Gran Chaco is the hottest and driest part of the nation, while the Paraneña is more humid.

Autumn and spring are somewhat milder. But at all times of the year, temperatures vary widely. Cold fronts alternate quickly with warm ones, sometimes causing quick and drastic temperature changes. Cold air masses move into Paraguay from the Antarctic region to the south, and warm air masses originate in the north, around the equator.

A **lapacho amarillo tree** flowers in the Gran Chaco. These trees do well in areas that receive little rain.

Paraguay's rainfall is generally abundant. Rain falls most heavily on the Paraná Plateau and lessens toward the west. It also varies seasonally, with the wettest period being from about November until April. Asunción averages about 55 inches (140 centimeters) per year. The only relatively dry region is in the northwestern corner of the Gran Chaco. In this area, the average rainfall is about 30 inches (76 cm) a year.

Flora and Fauna

Paraguay's vegetation—like its rainfall—is densest in the east. In that part of the country, semideciduous forests (whose trees lose only some of their leaves each year) cover the hills. Tall, broad-leaved trees are thickest in the Paraneña Plateau and its humid valleys. Some of the trees here are evergreens, which keep their leaves all year. Between the plateau and the Paraguay River, open savanna, with coarse grass and patches of palms, extends across the land. A species of holly grows wild in this region. Its leaves provide Paraguay's national beverage, yerba maté (holly tea). During rainy seasons, Paraguay's broad rivers sometimes support floating islands of matted plants, such as water hyacinths. Flowers of many colors cover these small islands.

In the Gran Chaco, leaf-shedding scrub woodlands thrive. They yield the commercially valuable quebracho tree. Tannin, a substance used in tanning (preparing) leather, comes from this hardwood. Toward the west, as rainfall decreases and thorn bushes and brush become more common, there are open areas of grassy savanna. During the dry season, patches of salty soil and small saltwater ponds appear in these open areas.

Animal life also abounds in Paraguay. Monkeys, jaguars, ocelots (medium-sized wildcats), deer, peccaries (wild pigs, also known as javelinas), and anteaters roam the Chaco. Tapirs are nocturnal (active at night) animals with hooves and short trunks that make Paraguay their home. Reptiles include poisonous coral snakes. Huge anacondas are snakes that live both on land and in water and sometimes reach 30 feet (9 m) in length.

The **yellow anaconda** is a smaller member of the anaconda family. These snakes can grow to be up to 12 feet (3.7 m) long.

The country's birdlife is varied. Kingfishers, bitterns (a heron-like marsh bird), snowy egrets, storks, and Muscovy ducks make the nation their home. Pheasants, quail, rheas (South American ostriches), and partridges are a few of the other native species.

Life thrives in Paraguay's many rivers, especially in the Paraguay River. Fish include the dorado (similar to salmon) and catfish. Among the most unusual native fish are lungfish, which bury themselves in mud to survive the dry season. Piranhas also swim the nation's waters. Piranhas are small but travel in large groups called schools. With their sharp teeth, they can reduce a deer that wanders into a river to a skeleton in a matter of minutes.

Paraguay's warm, humid climate is perfect for numerous insects. Many of these creatures bother and even endanger people and animals. For example, anopheles mosquitoes carry malaria—a tropical disease that threatens Paraguayans. Gnats cause skin irritations and infection. Fly larvae and several varieties of ticks bury themselves under the skin of humans and animals, resulting in sores and swellings. A small parasitic flea known as a chigger, or a pique, can bore into the tough soles of feet. Farmers must contend with insect pests, including leaf-cutting ants and boll weevils, which can cause severe crop damage.

NOT YOUR AVERAGE RODENT

One of Paraguay's unique animals is the capybara—the largest rodent in the world. Capybaras are semiaquatic, meaning that they spend some of their time in the water. Their slightly webbed feet help them move around in Paraguay's rivers.

These tailless, plant-eating animals are related to guinea pigs but weigh about seventy times as much. Adults weigh up to 140 pounds (64 kilograms) and can grow to be more than 4 feet (1.2 m) long. And the modern capybara is just a smaller cousin to giant capybaras, which lived more than ten thousand years ago. These extinct creatures were the size of grizzly bears. Some weighed more than 1,000 pounds (454 kg)!

The **Itaipú Dam** lies on the Alto Paraná River on the border between Paraguay and Brazil.

Natural Resources and Environmental Challenges

In contrast to its abundant wildlife, Paraguay has relatively few natural resources. In 2006 researchers found oil and natural gas in the northern Gran Chaco. But these valuable resources were in small amounts. In addition, because of the region's harsh terrain, they would be difficult to reach. The hunt for oil and gas in Paraguay had reached a dead end, at least for the time being.

But Paraguay does have some sources of fuel. Paraguay's many rivers create power in hydroelectric plants. Paraguay also holds peat, a natural material that forms as plants decay. People can burn peat, much like coal, to produce heat and other energy.

In addition, people use Paraguay's sandstone, limestone, and clay to make bricks and tiles. Extensive, potentially valuable deposits of marble and serpentine (a mineral used in industry as a source of magnesium and in architecture as a decorative stone) also exist. And Paraguay holds manganese and copper reserves, as well as small deposits of iron ore. These resources have not yet been widely mined.

Paraguay's natural setting is one of its great resources. But the nation faces several serious environmental problems. Deforestation—cutting down Paraguay's thick forests—is a growing issue. Pollution of the country's rivers, swamps, and other wetlands is another major concern. This pollution comes from industry and also from farmers' use of pesticides (chemicals to kill insects). Poaching—the illegal hunting of animals—is another problem. The nation's government has pledged to protect the environment, and the country contains several national parks and wildlife reserves. But progress has been slow. Environmental agencies are calling for stricter regulations and greater enforcement.

Cities

Paraguay's biggest population centers are in the east. The nation's capital, Asunción, is in southern Paraguay, close to the western border with Argentina.

ASUNCIÓN (population 1.5 million) rises from the banks of the Paraguay River and climbs the slopes of a low hill. Spanish settlers founded the city in 1537. Ever since then, it has been an important center. It is the nation's government seat and most important commercial city. Asunción is the hub of an urban area extending about 60 miles (97 km) from the city itself. This area is sometimes called Gran Asunción, or Greater Asunción. More than 1.5 million people live in Gran Asunción.

Asunción is one of the oldest cities in South America.

Asunción is a bustling city that combines modern life with a rich history. The bulk of the country's commerce passes through the old white Customs House, a landmark since colonial days. At docks along the Paraguay River, giant cranes load and unload supplies.

From the air, the city offers a view of red-tiled roofs, broad streets, green expanses, and patches of bright flowers. A few Spanish-style buildings survive from the colonial period. They feature grilled windows and rooms built around central patios. The city itself also follows a Spanish design, with rectangular blocks laid out around a central plaza.

> Visit www.vgsbooks.com for links to websites with additional information about Paraguay's cities.

CIUDAD DEL ESTE (population 321,000) is the second-largest city in Paraguay. It lies in far eastern Paraguay along the Alto Paraná River and very near the Brazilian border. The city was formerly named Puerto Flor del Lis and then Puerto Presidente Stroessner. It was founded in 1957, partly to house people building the Itaipú Dam. Until the dam's completion in 1981, this was the fastest-growing city in Paraguay.

ENCARNACIÓN (population estimated to be between 70,000 and 100,000) lies southwest of Ciudad del Este on the Alto Paraná River. After a tornado destroyed the city in 1926, Paraguayans rebuilt Encarnación. It is one of the nation's most modern towns. At the end of the Central Paraguayan Railroad, Encarnación is an active river port. In addition, good roads lead northeast to Iguazu Falls and northwest to Asunción. Trains move by ferryboat across the Alto Paraná River at Encarnación to continue on to Buenos Aires, the Argentine capital.

CONCEPCIÓN (population 76,000) is located about 200 miles (322 km) north of Asunción, on the Paraguay River. Trade with Brazil—including trade in cattle, hides, lumber, quebracho, tobacco, and yerba maté—passes through the town.

VILLARRICA (population 50,000) is centrally located in eastern Paraguay and boasts a colonial cathedral. Villarrica is also a marketing hub for cotton, tobacco, sugar, yerba maté, hides, meat, and domestic wines.

HISTORY AND GOVERNMENT

Humans began settling in South America and the region that became Paraguay as early as ten thousand to fifteen thousand years ago. These early peoples were hunters and gatherers who often moved from place to place in search of food and water.

The first inhabitants of Paraguay were followed by the indigenous Guarani people. This group formed communities in Paraguay and other parts of South America. Because they had no written language, no documents about their early history exist. But evidence reveals some facts about these people. For example, they were less nomadic than their ancestors had been. They formed villages where they grew crops including corn and manioc (a starchy root also called cassava). They also fished and hunted.

The Guarani belief system included a number of gods and goddesses. They told stories about these deities, and the stories passed from generation to generation. The Guarani also passed down other cultural and historical information through storytelling.

Founding of Asunción

Europeans first reached the New World of the Americas in the fifteenth century. The Italian explorer Christopher Columbus arrived in 1492. Columbus's expedition was on behalf of Spain, and Spanish adventurers and settlers soon followed. In 1516 Juan Díaz de Solís sailed up the Río de la Plata to the intersection of the Paraná and Uruguay rivers. He and most of his party died there during an attack launched by local peoples, but others continued the exploration into South America's interior. In the 1520s, the Portuguese explorer Alejo García reached the area that would later become Paraguay.

Spanish settlers established Asunción in 1537. It began as a fort, mostly to guard against competing Europeans who were also founding colonies in the region. Two main factors determined Asunción's location—its nearness to the Paraguay River and its setting in a valley with good farmland. In addition, Spanish visitors to the area had not come into conflict with the local people as they had in some parts of South America.

The site proved to be a good choice. Asunción flourished. Within twenty years of its founding, 1,500 Spanish families had settled there. They built a cathedral and a textile mill and began to raise cattle. Asunción would remain the most important center of Spanish power within the Río de la Plata area for nearly two centuries.

Asunción also played a central role in the Spanish Empire's growth. Groups set out from the settlement to explore, colonize, and use the land and resources of much of southern South America. These expeditions went on to settle northern and western Argentina, as well as the territories that became the nations of Bolivia and Uruguay.

Jesuit Settlements

In 1588 members of the Roman Catholic Society of Jesus, known as the Jesuits, arrived in Paraguay. Roman Catholicism is the religion of Spain. The Jesuits and other missionaries (religious workers) wanted to bring this branch of Christianity to the native inhabitants of Paraguay and other parts of Spain's New World empire. Of the several groups of missionaries in the area, the Jesuits soon became the most important.

By the end of the sixteenth century, the Jesuits had gathered about one hundred thousand Guarani people in Paraguay into agricultural colonies called *reducciones*. Forming the Paraguayan reducciones took place fairly peacefully. Many Guarani came to the Jesuit missions to escape slavery. Colonists and other people in the region were attacking

Guarani people use ladders and slings to harvest honey in Paraguay. A Jesuit priest drew this picture in the first half of the seventeenth century.

Founded in 1706 near the future site of Encarnación, the Jesuit mission of Trinidad was one of the last agricultural colonies to be built.

and capturing indigenous people to sell them as slaves. But the Jesuits benefited from the labor of the Guarani. They did farming, building, and other work that helped make the reducciones and their leaders wealthy. At the same time, the Jesuits worked to convert the Guarani to Christianity.

During this period, the Guarani did keep parts of their culture alive. They continued to speak their native language. They also maintained some of their traditional beliefs.

Spanish leaders eventually feared that the Jesuits were becoming too powerful. In 1767 the king of Spain officially expelled the Jesuits from Spanish colonies in Paraguay and elsewhere in the Americas. The reducciones fell into ruin, and the Guarani dispersed.

Neglect from Imperial Spain

Paraguay entered a period of imperial neglect. Eventually, officials in Spain formed plans to tighten the administration of its empire, which had grown too large for centralized control.

In 1776 Spain made Paraguay a province in the newly established Viceroyalty of the Río de la Plata. A viceroyalty is a territory governed by an official who acts on behalf of a colonizing nation's ruler. This power-ful state had its capital in Buenos Aires (later the capital of Argentina). Paraguayans resented their new status as a relatively low-ranking part of a larger body. They could do little to change things, however, since Buenos Aires controlled the Paraná River's mouth and therefore Paraguay's access to world markets. In the late eighteenth and early nineteenth centuries, Spanish rulers, who were busy with wars close to home, almost completely neglected Paraguay.

At this time, some Paraguayans were wealthy. They owned land and were often well educated. Primarily Spanish-born, many of them held positions in the colonial government. But many more people were poor. They could not afford to buy land. The gap dividing these groups was large.

Independence and Afterward

In the early 1800s, a series of wars in Europe weakened Spain. Its grip over many of its South American colonies began to slip as those territories began pushing for independence. Paraguay was one of them. One of the most prominent leaders in the colony was José Gaspar Rodríguez de Francia. Francia was a student of history and religion and widely considered the country's most highly educated man.

In 1811 Paraguay declared independence. Francia and other leaders were careful to seek their independence from Buenos Aires as well as from Spain. With their resources and power already strained, Spain could do little to stand in the way of Paraguayan freedom. The recently independent viceroyalty of Río de la Plata was a separate challenge. Still headquartered in Buenos Aires, the viceroyalty hoped to hold onto Paraguay's territory. But Paraguayan forces soon warded off an attempted takeover by Buenos Aires and also overthrew the remaining representatives of Spain in the colony. Paraguay officially achieved national independence on May 15, 1811.

Francia took control of the nation that same year. He soon emerged as a dictator who governed the country almost single-handedly. Francia's goals as leader included making Paraguay self-sufficient and ending foreign influence. In search of this goal, he cut off nearly all trade and contacts with the outside world. At the same time, he took power away from the Roman Catholic Church, which was wealthy and influential. The church also owned a lot of land in the country and beyond. Francia dissolved Catholic monasteries (communities of people, such as monks, who follow religious vows) in Paraguay. He also took some of the church's land and rented it to poor Paraguayans. But the gap between rich and poor remained very large.

During the reign of José Gaspar Rodríguez de Francia, his title was El Supremo Dictador (the Supreme Dictator).

To support his government, Francia depended on the army, the police, and a huge number of informers and spies. He divided the country into military districts and let the efficient and disciplined army control the countryside. The police were put in charge of the towns. He repressed all who opposed him—and even many of those whom he thought might present opposition. He forced native peoples and mestizos (people with mixed indigenous and Spanish ancestry) to work for the government as farmers, ranchers, and road builders.

In keeping with his aim of self-sufficiency, Francia introduced improved agricultural technology and developed local industries. He hoped that these changes would end the need for imported goods and for contact with the outside world. In addition, no one was allowed to leave the country.

During his time as dictator, Francia did not set up any lasting governmental systems, such as a constitution or a congress. As a result, disorder followed his death in 1840. Francia had left Paraguay's people with neither the resources nor the experience necessary for self-government. However, Francia also left behind a unified people with strong national pride.

◉ A Different Kind of Dictator

A military junta (ruling group) temporarily took power after Francia's death. This ruling council included Carlos Antonio López. López was a wealthy rancher as well as an expert in law. He soon emerged as his nation's new leader. Beginning in 1841, he governed as one of two officials called consuls. And in 1844, López became president of Paraguay.

López was Francia's nephew, but he had not been Francia's political ally. He soon reversed most of Francia's policies. López reopened Paraguayan ports to trade and restored some of the Catholic Church's power. And unlike his solitary uncle, López surrounded himself with advisers. They helped him put into place a system of laws that he himself had written.

Carlos Antonio López

López administered his government well and won the support of most of the country's wealthy and politically influential people. But López also kept a tight grip on his position and its control of the government. The constitution he introduced gave the president a great deal of power and did not include protections for civil rights. But while López was as dictatorial as Francia had been, his policies were milder and led to improved conditions in Paraguay.

One of López's most important moves was to begin the process of abolishing slavery. Slavery in Paraguay dated back to its early colonial days. Spanish colonists had brought a small number of African slaves to the New World. Most of these slaves worked in colonial homes. As time went on, colonists throughout the region had also forced thousands of native Guarani into slavery. And beginning in the eighteenth century, the Spanish brought about fifty thousand slaves from Africa to the colony. Most of these slaves worked on farms. The African slave trade continued into the nineteenth century.

López introduced a law that ended the slave trade. But the law did not free people who were already slaves. Instead, it ensured that the children of slaves would be freed when they reached the age of twenty-five. Slavery would not be completely abolished in Paraguay until 1869.

López's other changes included promoting education by founding elementary schools. He established a newspaper, promoted trade, and introduced additional modern agricultural techniques. López also built a railway, developed the nation's road system, bridged rivers, and opened up the Paraguay River to steam navigation. When López died in 1862, Paraguay was a fairly prosperous nation. But its population did not share the wealth evenly. Many people still did not own any land, while a few citizens held large amounts of property. And most of the country's people did not enjoy broad liberties.

Francisco Solano López and the War of the Triple Alliance

Paraguay's third dictator was Carlos Antonio López's son, Francisco Solano López. The older López had planned for his son to follow him as president. He had appointed him to several important military positions in his government, including minister of war. As minister of war, López gained experience serving as a Paraguayan representative in Europe. The young López came to see himself as a military genius.

Francisco Solano López was president of Paraguay from 1862 to 1870.

Brazilian forces repel Paraguayan soldiers at the Paraná River in 1866 during the **War of the Triple Alliance.**

As planned, López became president after his father's death. He soon had a chance to use his military experience. In 1864, when Brazilian troops intervened in a revolution in Uruguay, López declared war on Brazil. In part, López feared Brazil was seeking military conquests that might include Paraguay. But he also was seeking conquests and glory of his own. When Argentina refused to let Paraguayan troops cross Argentine territory to reach southern Brazil, López declared war on Argentina as well. In 1865 Uruguay—influenced by Brazil—joined Brazil and Argentina. The three nations formed a triple alliance against Paraguay. The War of the Triple Alliance lasted for five years. Paraguayans fought bravely, but they were outnumbered and overpowered. The conflict ended in 1870, when López was killed and Paraguay surrendered.

By the time this devastating war drew to a close, it had killed more than half of Paraguay's people. And according to the terms of the peace treaty that ended the conflict, Paraguay lost about 55,000 square miles (142,449 sq. km) of its territory. The war also left Paraguay with a huge debt that it could not pay off. Some observers questioned whether the badly weakened country would be able to maintain its independence—especially when Brazilian and Argentine troops remained to occupy the nation for several years. It seemed possible that either Brazil or Argentina might attempt to overtake the small nation lying between them. But although they'd won the war, both Brazil and Argentina had suffered their own losses. Paraguay continued to cling to its independence.

MILITARY LIFE

For forty years after the War of the Triple Alliance, Paraguay had almost no military forces. This lack was a radical change for a people who historically had spent much of their national treasure for defense. The military uniform became an object of contempt, and Paraguay's remaining army consisted of a handful of poorly disciplined draftees.

An Uneasy Freedom

In the 1870s and 1880s, two main political parties emerged in Paraguay. General Bernardino Caballero, a hero of the War of the Triple Alliance, founded and led a party called the Colorados (meaning "Reds") in Paraguay. Their political rival was the Liberal Party.

The Colorados dominated Paraguayan politics for the next several decades. During this period, Caballero was a powerful figure with great influence over who did and did not become president. He himself held the office from 1881 through 1886. During this period, the opposing Liberal Party had little influence.

In the final months of 1904, however, the Liberals gained power when Paraguay's army overthrew the then president Juan Antonio Escurra. Liberal Party member Juan Bautista Gaona became president. One of the goals of the Liberals once they had power was to rebuild and strengthen Paraguay's military, which had never recovered from the War of the Triple Alliance. The Liberals started a military school, organized military units with modern equipment, and began to enlist men for the nation's armed services. Beginning in 1909, Paraguayan men were required to serve in the military, and in 1912, leaders reorganized the army's structure.

But despite these efforts, the Liberals were not able to restore political stability. The first eight years of Liberal Party rule saw ten presidents—four in 1911 alone. Until 1932 presidents served an average of only about two years before being thrown out by rivals. Revolutions became a regular part of Paraguay's national life. But none involved major political or economic issues. Almost without exception, these revolutions resulted from the conflict between personal egos or from political rivalry.

Paraguayans learned to live with political instability during this tumultuous period. Despite the turmoil in the capital city, economic development continued in rural areas. Farming and ranching expanded and became more modern. Industries arose and transportation routes were improved. Slow but steady progress took place in health and public education. And Paraguay was unaffected by World War I (1914–1918), a conflict among several European powers.

A man harvests sugarcane in Paraguay in the early 1900s. Sugarcane became one of the country's major exports in the twentieth century.

At the same time, the government had been encouraging immigrants to move to Paraguay. Paraguayan leaders were eager to increase the nation's population, which was still drastically low due to the war. Most of these immigrants came from Europe (especially Italy, Germany, France, and Spain) and the Middle East. Some also came from Argentina and other South American nations. These arrivals brought in valuable foreign investment, as well as new technology. Paraguay was soon producing high agricultural yields. Its crops included cotton, tobacco, corn, coffee, sugarcane, manioc, rice, and citrus fruits. The nation also increased its production of valuable forest products such as rubber and yerba maté.

Large corporations also played an important role in settling and developing the land. For instance, French, British, and U.S. companies developed the export of yerba maté and timber. Between the late 1800s and early 1900s, investment in Paraguay boomed. This income was valuable. But it came at a high price of its own, as foreign companies took control of the nation's best farmlands and natural resources.

◉ The Chaco War

Meanwhile, a bigger issue was brewing. Since colonial days, Paraguay and Bolivia had both claimed control over the wild Gran Chaco region. But for many decades, few people thought much about who held this huge but mostly empty stretch of wilderness.

Paraguayan troops carry supplies to the front lines during the **Chaco War** (1932–1935).

In the final years of the nineteenth century, however, new factors came into play. Suddenly, ownership of the Chaco became a matter of intense interest to both Paraguay and Bolivia. Paraguay saw expanding its territory as a good way to restore the national pride it had lost in the War of the Triple Alliance. Bolivia, on the other hand, had lost its access to the Pacific Ocean to Chile in 1883. Access to the Gran Chaco's Paraguay River would give Bolivia a route to the Atlantic Ocean via the Río de la Plata.

Bolivia and Paraguay both used the Gran Chaco dispute as a reason to expand and modernize their militaries. Other nations soon got involved as well. Chilean leaders supported Bolivia, while Argentina backed Paraguay. Rumors of vast petroleum (oil) deposits in the Gran Chaco fueled the competition even further.

In 1928 a Paraguayan force attacked a Bolivian outpost. The incident touched off a storm of accusations and counterattacks. The Paraguayan government accused the Standard Oil Company, located in New Jersey, of financing Bolivia's buildup of new weapons. Bolivian officials charged that Great Britain and Argentina were secretly helping Paraguay.

The size and violence of incidents gradually grew, exploding into full-blown war by 1932. With three times the population of Paraguay, greater wealth, and a German-trained army, Bolivia seemed likely to overwhelm its weaker opponent. But Bolivia's government was unstable and corrupt. And Bolivian troops, accustomed to high altitudes, found it difficult to fight in the Gran Chaco's swampy lowlands.

Paraguay, in contrast, had an able president at the time—Eusebio Ayala. It also had a competent military leader named José Félix Estigarribia. In addition, the Paraguayan people were more committed to the fight than most Bolivians. Paraguayans felt that they were defending their homeland. And most international observers sided with Paraguay, making it easier for Paraguay's government to purchase arms and supplies from foreign powers.

Altogether, about one hundred thousand troops took part in the Chaco War. It was a long and grueling conflict. During the rainy season, soldiers often fought in deep mud. During the dry season, they frequently struggled to find drinking water. Disease killed as many people as actual combat. The war dragged on for three years before hostilities finally came to a halt. Paraguay and Bolivia agreed to a cease-fire in 1935. In 1938 a formal peace treaty confirmed Paraguay's victory and awarded the nation more than 20,000 square miles (51,800 sq. km) of land.

A Series of Dictators

After the Chaco War, several Paraguayan leaders rose to power based on the roles—often exaggerated—they had played in the war. One was General José Félix Estigarribia. Estigarribia became president on August 15, 1939. The general soon created yet another dictatorship. But his pledge to improve the welfare of the people and to boost the country's prosperity won him widespread support. In 1940 Estigarribia introduced a new constitution that set forth these ideals.

But in September 1940, Estigarribia died in an airplane crash. Higinio Morínigo—another veteran of the Chaco War—became president. Morínigo was a less humane leader than Estigarribia. Morínigo immediately suspended the constitution and began to reshape the government. Soon he had concentrated power in his hands. Rejecting democratic principles, Morínigo presided over the nation as a dictator. His one-man rule would last eight years.

Higinio Morínigo served as Paraguay's minister of war before he became president in 1940.

During that reign, Morínigo's administration crushed attempts at revolt and imprisoned huge numbers of people who protested against the harsh dictatorship. The outbreak of World War II (1939–1945) in Europe and Asia only benefited Morínigo. He used it as an excuse to keep a tight grip on his own country. In addition, the war brought financial benefits to Paraguay. Shortages of goods elsewhere led to increased demand and higher prices for Paraguay's exports of beef, hides, cotton, and quebracho. At the same time, Paraguay borrowed money from other nations. These loans helped build roads, start industries, and reequip the military.

In international affairs, Morínigo followed the lead of the United States. He broke off relations with the war's Axis (pro-German) powers in 1942. He declared war against them in 1944—by which time it was obvious that the Allies (the countries fighting against Germany) would win. He also signed the Charter of the United Nations after the war. This treaty founded the United Nations, an international organization to help handle global disputes. During the war, however, Morínigo had provided refuge for Axis spies, protected their activities, promoted discrimination against Jews, and suppressed demonstrations that supported the Allies.

Visit www.vgsbooks.com for links to websites with additional information about the history of Paraguay, including the country's growth during and after World War II.

Throughout these years, opposition to Morínigo had grown steadily. Strikes (work stoppages) and student riots broke out periodically to protest the government's policies. The unrest escalated in March 1947, when a rebel named Rafael Franco led a revolt that erupted into a civil war. Many members of the military sided with the rebellion. But Morínigo had the support of the Colorados and used their power to crush the rebels. Morínigo regained control in August 1947.

Morínigo's troubles were not over, however. The Colorados were facing disagreements and power struggles among themselves. By the end of 1947, one faction of the Colorado Party forced Morínigo to leave the country. In early 1948, Colorado Party member Juan Natalicio González won an election. He had appeared alone on the ballot. But after a number of uprisings, a rival faction of the Colorado Party, led by Federico Chávez, assumed control in 1950.

Chávez continued Morínigo's severe policies. But his rule was unstable. The nation's people remained angry and eager for change.

Alfredo Stroessner joined the army at the age of sixteen. He reached the rank of general in 1948.

On top of years of political turmoil, the population had endured economic hardships. The country's economy was in a shambles after several wars and a host of harsh leaders. Poverty continued to plague many of the nation's people. In July 1954, a military officer named General Alfredo Stroessner led a coup (seizure of power) that overthrew Chávez. Stroessner was elected to the nation's presidency without opposition on July 11, 1954.

Stroessner's Rise and Fall

The son of a German immigrant father and a Paraguayan mother, Alfredo Stroessner seemed to represent change. After all, he had overthrown a harsh and unpopular leader. But in fact, Stroessner was yet another dictator. He and the Colorado Party ran the Paraguayan government by restricting people's rights, arresting people who spoke against the government, and using military force.

Stroessner did follow some policies that helped his nation. For example, Stroessner maintained good relations with the governments of Argentina and Brazil. Paraguay's economy was closely linked with these two powerful nations. Stroessner went on to seek and receive Brazilian financial support in the construction of the Itaipú Dam on the Alto Paraná River. At the time, the dam was the world's largest source of hydroelectric energy.

Stroessner also benefited from a strong friendship with the United States. The U.S. government helped build the first all-weather road across the Chaco region, supplied experts to help modernize Paraguay's farms, and gave assistance to schools and public health facilities.

Throughout Stroessner's reign, his administration paid the most attention to Asunción—the area with the most people. As a result, most of the development funds that came in from the United States and elsewhere benefited wealthy residents of the capital. Meanwhile, most of the nation's rural citizens remained without basic modern conveniences, such as plumbing and electricity. So while Paraguay experienced economic growth under Stroessner, only a small group of wealthy Paraguayans enjoyed the rewards.

Furthermore, the stability of Stroessner's long rule came at great cost to the political rights and individual freedoms of Paraguayans. Opponents of the regime were arrested, kidnapped, exiled, tortured, or murdered. And while Stroessner won a total of eight consecutive elections, they were rigged in his favor. In reality, no opponent ever had the chance to take power. Stroessner allowed an opposition candidate to appear on Paraguay's election ballots only in the years 1963 and 1988.

In the late 1980s, the elderly Stroessner began to leave day-to-day operations to his aides. But the question of who would become the next president caused a split in the ruling Colorado Party. This division prompted General Andrés Rodríguez, second in command of the army after Stroessner, to take power in a violent coup in February 1989. Stroessner later went into exile in Brazil.

◉ Changes and Challenges

Stroessner's fall brought demands for political reform. Many people wanted the nation's leaders to become more independent of the military. In June 1992, a group called

COLD FRONT

Why did the U.S. government have a friendly relationship with a dictator such as Stroessner? The answer lies in a conflict between the United States and the Soviet Union, called the Cold War (1945–1991). This political conflict was fierce but never erupted into a "hot" (military) war between the two superpowers. During the Cold War, Communist and non-Communist forces struggled to gain power and influence throughout the world. Communism is a political, social, and economic system based on the idea of common, rather than private, property. In a Communist system, the government controls land, resources, industry, and money and distributes them among its citizens. U.S. leaders did not want Communism to spread around the world, particularly in South and Central America. They feared that if Communist governments took power there, they would give the Soviet Union influence over the region. Stroessner, was also against Communism, so U.S. leaders worked to make him an ally.

a constituent assembly drew up a new Paraguayan constitution. The document barred General Rodríguez from running again for the presidency. The constitution also created a new post of vice president and expanded the Supreme Court from five to nine members.

At the same time, strong disagreements remained among the Colorados. Some people—including the powerful military—favored Stroessner's old policies. Their opponents, on the other hand, pushed for new civilian (nonmilitary) leaders and further reforms. After a bitterly fought election, the pro-reform Juan Carlos Wasmosy emerged as Colorado Party leader in March 1993.

In May 1993, Wasmosy won Paraguay's first free presidential election, in which all voters were free to vote for the candidate of their choice. Wasmosy privatized (sold) many state-owned industries. He also opened up Paraguay's economy to more foreign trade and investment.

In 1998 Raúl Cubas Grau was elected president, continuing the Colorados's political domination. Cubas Grau pledged to cut government spending, help the nation's poor and rural residents, and lessen government corruption. But his lofty goals soon fell by the wayside as dissent broke out within the Colorados once again. The attempts of Cubas Grau's opponents to remove him from office failed. However, disagreements among government members prevented them from addressing serious issues such as the nation's economy.

Events took a violent turn in March 1999. Supporters of a political rival of Cubas Grau assassinated Luis María Argaña, Cubas Grau's vice president. Soon afterward, Cubas Grau resigned under great pressure from his rivals.

Luis González Macchi became Paraguay's next president. One of his early moves was to reorganize the military—partly by removing many officers from their positions. This move was not a popular change, and in May 2000, a group of soldiers attempted a coup. Macchi's forces defeated the attempted overthrow, and the government declared a

A TERRIBLE DISCOVERY

In 1992 several men—including a lawyer, a human-rights activist, and a judge—were in an Asunción police station. They were searching for files on a prisoner. They did find files—but not the ones they were looking for. Instead, they stumbled on a huge archive of documents describing details about thousands of people who had been arrested, tortured, and murdered in Paraguay under Alfredo Stroessner's regime, as well as in other dictator-run South and Central American nations during the same period. These files became known as the Archives of Terror.

state of emergency that gave Macchi broader powers than ever. Many citizens were arrested in the coup's wake. Macchi went on to survive several more attempts to force him from the presidency, as well as numerous worker strikes and protests against his government.

In August 2003, Nicanor Duarte Frutos—yet another Colorado leader—succeeded Macchi. His promises to voters included lessening corruption and strengthening the still-struggling economy. With the former goal in mind, he removed several Supreme Court judges suspected of corruption from their posts.

Like previous leaders, Duarte faced a variety of challenges. One ongoing issue was the uneven distribution of land. This problem has troubled Paraguay for many decades. Beginning in 2003, indigenous groups and farmers staged a series of uprisings. They demanded that the government distribute farmland to the country's landless farmers, as well as to poor indigenous Paraguayans. The protesters launched strikes and marches, set up roadblocks, and illegally occupied some of the disputed lands. While Duarte agreed to give the protesting groups some land, he did not fully meet their demands. The matter has still not been completely resolved.

Several nonpolitical crises also marred these years. Tragedy struck in August 2004, when a fire at an Asunción supermarket killed more than 420 people. And in 2007, a severe outbreak of dengue fever (a virus spread by mosquitoes) erupted. The disease affected more than 25,000 people, straining the country's medical system. That same year, raging fires destroyed more than 375 square miles (971 sq. km) of forest and farmland in the northern Paraneña.

Firefighters struggle to put out a deadly fire at a supermarket in Asunción in 2004. A gas leak caused the fire.

In April 2008, former Roman Catholic bishop Fernando Lugo was elected president. Lugo was a member of the Patriotic Alliance for Change political party. His election ended more than sixty years of Colorado control in Paraguay. Lugo took office in April 2008, promising voters that he would address corruption and reduce the economic inequality that still troubles the country.

Government

Paraguay's 1992 constitution established three independent branches of government—executive, legislative, and judiciary. Voters elect the president (the head of the executive branch) to a single five-year term. All citizens over the age of eighteen are eligible to vote. The president relies on a vice president and a council of ministers (whom the president appoints) for advice and assistance in governing.

Voters also elect legislators to five-year terms. The country's bicameral (two-house legislature) consists of a forty-five-member senate and an eighty-member chamber of deputies. The senate writes laws concerning national defense and treaties, while the chamber of deputies is responsible for legislation affecting internal matters.

Paraguay's highest court is the Supreme Court composed of a chief justice and eight associate justices. The president appoints these judges, who serve five-year terms. Special appeals courts decide criminal, civil, and labor cases, and civil courts handle commercial cases.

The country is divided into seventeen administrative departments (provinces). An elected governor heads each one.

AN INDIGENOUS VOICE

In 2008 Margarita Mbywangi became the minister for indigenous affairs in Paraguay's government. Although this minister oversees matters that affect the country's indigenous population, Mbywangi is the first indigenous person to hold the office. Some of her goals include reducing poverty and helping more indigenous people own their own land.

THE PEOPLE

Paraguay is home to 6.2 million people. Its population density is 39 people per square mile (15 per sq. km). In comparison, in Paraguay's neighbor Brazil, about 60 people live in every square mile (23 per sq. km). The United States has a density of 83 people per square mile (32 per sq. km). But Paraguay's population is not evenly distributed around the country. It is concentrated in the eastern part of the nation, especially in and around Asunción. About 57 percent of Paraguayans live in urban areas.

The Paraguayan population is increasing at a rate of about 2.1 percent annually—faster than the South American average of 1.4 percent each year. If the population continues to grow at this rate, it will reach about 8 million by the year 2025.

A major issue facing the nation is poverty. About one-third to one-half of all Paraguayans must struggle to afford basic food, shelter, and other necessities. Poverty rates are higher in rural areas than in cities. And the gap between the country's rich and poor is extremely large.

Ethnic Groups

The vast majority of Paraguay's people are mestizos. With mixed indigenous and European (mostly Spanish) heritage, mestizos make up about 95 percent of all Paraguayans.

A range of other ethnic groups comprise the remaining 5 percent of Paraguayans. A very small number of people have entirely native heritage. Most of them are Guarani or members of Guarani subgroups, but others belong to different indigenous peoples. They live mainly in the Chaco and in the northeastern part of the country.

Paraguay also has a small black population. Most of them are descendants of African slaves brought to the colony between the 1500s and 1700s.

Paraguay is home to immigrants from Europe, the Middle East, and Asia. Many Japanese people have immigrated to Paraguay, especially during World War II. Most Japanese Paraguayans live in agricultural communities in the southern part of the country around Encarnación.

Pedestrians and drivers crowd a street in Ciudad del Este.

◉ Daily Life

Daily life for Paraguayans varies widely between city and country dwellers. In general, townspeople are considered to have higher status than country folk. Those who live in Asunción, in turn, tend to have higher social status than those who live in smaller towns.

City dwellers generally live in small but comfortable houses made of brick or stucco (a type of plaster) and covered with tiled roofs. These homes are usually painted cheerful pastel colors. Many poor urban residents live in shacks, often on the edges of towns. In contrast, housing for the rich is spacious. Wealthy Paraguayans have heat, electricity, and indoor plumbing.

People in urban areas dress in similar styles as North Americans or Europeans, with men wearing trousers and shirts or suits and women wearing slacks or skirts with shirts. They usually work in offices or shops. In Asunción many people work for the government.

Most rural Paraguayans are farmers. A few are wealthy ranchers who own large estates. But most people own only small plots of land, while others cultivate tracts that do not belong to them. Some of these landless farmers turn over part of their crop to the landowner, and some pay rent for the use of the land. Others simply farm unused soil without permission. They work it until its productivity declines (about every two or three years). Then they move on to another place. Most of these farmers work long, hard days. Many use simple hand tools and ox-drawn plows. Some grow only enough food to feed their own families, while others raise enough to sell crops at markets. In addition to farming, many rural residents have other trades or specialties. They may work as shepherds or truck drivers. Others saw logs, make charcoal, or do handicrafts such as making straw hats.

To add to their small income, some rural Paraguayans catch wild monkeys to sell as pets. Monkeys that have not been sold sometimes serve a practical function. Farmers dress the animals in red suits and turn them loose to frighten other monkeys away from crops.

Rural Paraguayans generally live in modest homes. Their houses are square structures known as ranchos. These buildings often consist of a single room. They are made of adobe (clay) or of stakes bound together or plastered with mud. Their floors are earth, clay, or brick, and roofs are usually thatched with dried grasses. The country's mild climate allows many low-income Paraguayans to keep their homes unheated, except for a cooking stove or fire. Indoor plumbing is also rare in much of rural Paraguay.

Many rural people wear modern clothing, such as T-shirts and jeans. But others choose more traditional garb, with men donning loose pants (*bombachas*) and shirts or jackets. Women often wear colorful knit shawls known as rebozos, paired with dresses or skirts. Men and women both wear ponchos (woven shoulder capes, with a hole in the center for the wearer's head).

A **farmer in rural Paraguay** uses an oxcart to carry his harvest to the market.

Family Ties and Women's Lives

Family has traditionally been an important focus of Paraguayan life. The typical Paraguayan family unit is large and includes distant relatives. Members of this extended family rely on one another for help, support, and advice in all areas of life.

Despite these historically strong ties, many families in modern Paraguay are fractured. Domestic violence is common, with many women suffering physical abuse at their husbands' hands.

Especially in rural Paraguay, marriage is frequently an informal affair—often without a religious or a legal ceremony. Partly as a consequence, ending such marriages isn't difficult, and spouses leave one another quite often. When marriages do break apart, the woman usually bears the burden of raising the children. Even when couples remain together, men are often away working as farmers or laborers. In addition to child rearing, women are responsible for most housework and chores, including grinding corn, cooking food, and mending clothes.

Paraguayan women also face challenges outside the home. Many encounter discrimination when they seek jobs and often receive lower pay than men. Sexual harassment in the workplace is a problem.

A **woman assembles a child's bicycle** at a factory in Asunción. Many Paraguayan women receive lower wages than men for doing the same work.

Another human rights concern in Paraguay is human trafficking. Traffickers move people across national borders for exploitation. Traffickers in Paraguay usually target poor women and children by promising them work in other countries. Once they are outside of Paraguay (usually in other South American nations), the traffickers force these people into unpaid or underpaid labor and prostitution.

 Visit www.vgsbooks.com for links to websites with additional information about the people of Paraguay, including efforts to improve access to health care and education.

Health

Only 1 doctor exists for every 1,000 people in the country. This figure is low compared to most nations. Most doctors—as well as most of the nation's nurses, dentists, and other health-care professionals—work in hospitals and clinics in Asunción. The situation is much worse in rural areas. Those clinics that do exist in the countryside and in small villages tend to be underequipped and badly understaffed. Furthermore, there are not enough programs to provide shots protecting children against disease.

Poverty—especially high in rural areas—poses another great challenge to the health and welfare of Paraguayans. Most people do not have health insurance. About 15 percent of the nation's people are undernourished. Lack of nourishing food makes them more likely to get sick.

The current life expectancy for Paraguayans is 71 years of age. Because the population is growing rapidly, it is young. More than one-third of all Paraguayans are under the age of 15. Paraguay's infant mortality rate is 36 deaths for every 1,000 live births. This number is high for South America, where the average is 23 per 1,000. Less than 1 percent of adults have the human immunodeficiency virus (HIV), which causes acquired immunodeficiency syndrome (AIDS).

Sicknesses affecting Paraguayans include measles, tuberculosis (a lung disease), and acute respiratory infections. Dysentery—an intestinal disease that causes vomiting, diarrhea, and fever—spreads through contaminated water. Hookworm is a parasite that feeds on human blood. It also spreads through water. About three-quarters of Paraguayans have access to good water sources, but cases of water-borne diseases still occur.

Insect-borne illnesses are another ongoing threat. Insects infect some Paraguayans with Chagas' disease, which damages the nervous

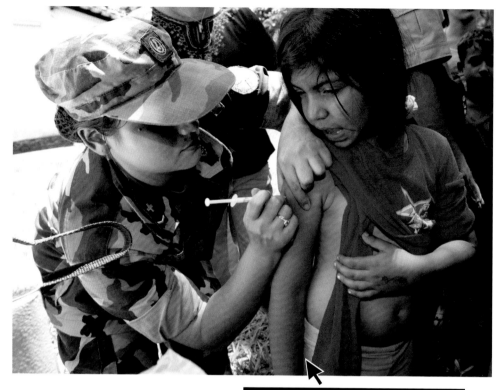

A government worker administers a **yellow fever and dengue fever vaccine** during a 2008 outbreak of the deadly diseases.

system and heart. Sandflies carry leishmaniasis, which can affect internal organs as well as the skin. Mosquitoes carry the tropical diseases dengue fever, malaria, and yellow fever. Widespread outbreaks of dengue fever in 2007 and of yellow fever in 2008 affected hundreds of people. The health system was not prepared for these outbreaks. In 2008 health-care providers did not have enough vaccines.

Many Paraguayans—both in the country and among Asunción residents who are poorer—treat their ailments with a variety of traditional folk cures. These homemade remedies are usually plant based, including herbs and other natural ingredients.

Education

Education in Paraguay is free and required for students in elementary school, which begins at the age of six or seven. The nation's enrollment rates for elementary school are high, with close to 90 percent of school-aged children attending early grades. Literacy rates are fairly high, with about 94 percent of the adult population able to read and write.

School enrollment drops sharply in secondary school, however, when many young people must give up their studies to work in the fields to help their families. Not enough schools exist to handle all eligible students. Education is especially inadequate in rural areas, where there are frequently not enough teachers or resources. Government spending on education has risen since 2000, but more progress is still necessary.

Paraguay offers technical and vocational education to young people, teaching them specific trades and skills. These programs have been popular with both students and parents.

Several universities and colleges provide higher education to Paraguayan students. The largest and oldest is the National University of Asunción, which dates back to 1890. This public school enrolls more than thirty thousand students. Our Lady of the Assumption Catholic University, a private school in Asunción, is another large institution. More than ten thousand students attend. Both of these universities have branches in cities and towns outside Asunción. They offer a variety of programs including instruction in engineering, medicine, agriculture, business, and veterinary science. Wealthy Paraguayans, however, often send their children to universities in Argentina and Brazil for higher education.

Girls work on a group project in a **secondary school in Asunción.**

CULTURAL LIFE

Paraguayans are deeply proud of their Guarani heritage. It appears in many aspects of the nation's cultural life. But Paraguay's Spanish colonial past has also shaped its modern culture. The blending of Guarani and Spanish influence shows up in music, dance, literature, religion, and social customs in Paraguay.

▷ Religion

The Roman Catholic faith has been important to Paraguayans since colonial times. The ruins of Jesuit missions remain as a reminder of Catholicism's history in the nation. Close to 90 percent of modern Paraguayans follow the religion.

About 6 percent of the population belongs to non-Catholic branches of Christianity. These include the Lutheran, Baptist, and Mormon churches. About thirty thousand Mennonites live in Paraguay. Mennonites are members of a Christian religion founded in sixteenth-century Netherlands. In the early 1900s, Mennonites moved to Paraguay from

Germany, Ukraine, Canada, and other nations. They were seeking freedom from prejudice. They also came in search of land. They found both in Paraguay—mostly in the wilderness lands of the Gran Chaco. There they established farming settlements and practiced their faith freely. Other communities sprang up in eastern Paraguay, but roughly half of modern Paraguayan Mennonites still live in the Chaco. One of the largest communities there is Menno Colony, founded by immigrants from Canada in the 1920s. It is home to close to ten thousand inhabitants.

Some Paraguayans combine Christianity with traditional beliefs. Guarani legends and folklore tell of many spirits with influence on human lives. For example, the Pombero is a short, ugly creature with hairy hands and feet who makes animal noises at night. The *pora* is the guardian of buried treasure, and the *yasi yatere* lures children into the deep woods when they are supposed to be napping. Paraguayans believe that they must respect these spirits in order to please them and keep them from harming humans or making mischief.

Catholics celebrate the Day of the Cross in Asunción in early May. During this holiday, people decorate public places with donuts made with tapioca flour. The donuts are given out as presents during the celebration.

The remaining 4 percent of Paraguayans includes small populations of Jews, Muslims, Buddhists, and followers of other religions. Some Paraguayans follow indigenous beliefs without combining them with Christianity. And some do not belong to any religion.

Holidays and Festivals

With Catholicism dominant in Paraguay, many of the country's biggest holidays are Christian. Christmas, on December 25, brings a festive spirit and warm weather. Flowers are everywhere, decorating homes and churches. Nativity scenes called *pesebres*, made up of figures re-creating the birth of Jesus in a manger, also appear. Traditionally, the figure of Jesus is added to the scene only on Christmas Eve.

Catholics attend a midnight Mass (Catholic church service) on Christmas Eve. This special service is called la Misa del Gallo, or Mass

ALFALFA FIESTA

Paraguay is home to a harvest festival called the Festival of Alfalfa. Held in Sapucaí, in southern Paraguay, this event celebrates the end of the alfalfa harvest. (Alfalfa is a grassy plant that is often used to feed animals.) Festivalgoers enjoy music and dancing at this cheerful gathering.

of the Rooster. Afterward, families return home to enjoy a festive late-night dinner. On Christmas Day, people may exchange gifts, visit friends, go out for meals such as *asado* (barbecued meat, usually beef), or even go dancing in the streets.

Easter celebrations in March or April begin during the Semana Santa (Holy Week) leading up to the holiday. Much of this week is a time for church services and prayer. Processions through the streets, accompanied by somber religious chants, also take place during this week. Easter Sunday is focused on family.

Paraguayans observe a number of secular (nonreligious) holidays, as well. Independence Day, on May 15, celebrates the nation's 1811 independence from Spain. People around the country enjoy parades, concerts, and fireworks. Mid-August brings a day celebrating the founding of Asunción.

Several of Paraguay's other national holidays mark events from the country's wars. Heroes' Day, on March 1, honors the service of Paraguayan soldiers in the War of the Triple Alliance. Boquerón Battle Victory Day on September 29 commemorates an early battle in the Chaco War.

A Paraguayan gaucho, or cowboy, competes at a rodeo held during a religious festival. Rodeos accompany many celebrations in Paraguay.

The Language of Daily Life

Unlike many indigenous tongues, Guarani is alive and well. Most Paraguayans speak the language at home. A few Guarani words follow below:

one	petei
two	mokoi
three	mbohapy
man	kuimba'e
woman	kuña
sun	kuarahy
moon	jasy

⊙ Language and Literature

Spanish and Guarani are both official languages in Paraguay, and most people speak both. The Guarani language continues to be the most widely spoken tongue. Typically, most people use Spanish for formal occasions or for business matters (especially international) but speak Guarani at home and in everyday matters. The country's constitution is written in both languages, as are most textbooks.

Guarani was also the language of the nation's first literature—but it was unwritten. Storytellers passed down Guarani myths by recounting them out loud. These myths included a creation legend and many stories about a host of gods, goddesses, and spirits.

During colonial times, Spanish settlers wrote many historical and legal studies. Most authors of these works held important government positions. In the late nineteenth century, a writer named Blas Garay produced four famous volumes on Paraguayan history. One described seventeenth- and eighteenth-century Jesuit missions. A few decades later, Juan Emiliano O'Leary composed works of poetry as well as history. His historical writings examined the War of the Triple Alliance and praised Francisco Solano López.

Since Paraguay won its independence, most of the nation's prominent writers have used the Guarani language for at least some of their works. Among modern writers of note is former president Juan Natalicio González, who wrote poetry as well as historical works in the early 1900s. Justo Pastor Benítez, a former minister of foreign affairs, wrote articles and essays on politics and history.

Other modern authors include Augusto Roa Bastos, who wrote novels, poetry, short stories, and more. Roa Bastos, who died in 2005, was not only one of the most important writers in Paraguay but in all South America. In 1989 he won the Cervantes Prize for Literature, a prestigious annual prize for Spanish-language authors. Roa Bastos also

Augusto Roa Bastos

used Guarani words, as well as traditional legends and themes, in his books. His best-known work is the 1974 novel *Yo el Supremo (I, the Supreme)*. Roa Bastos wrote it from the point of view of former Paraguayan dictator José Gaspar Rodríguez de Francia.

Renée Ferrer de Arréllaga is a prominent poet and novelist. She has been publishing work since the 1960s. Susy Delgado is a poet who writes in both Spanish and Guarani. Her first novel, *La Sangre Florecida* (The blowered blood), appeared in 2002.

◑ Visual Arts

Early Guarani art in Paraguay included masks and carved wood. Much of this art depicted the country's wildlife, such as a carved wooden fish with a wide-open mouth.

Some of Paraguay's other oldest arts are traditional crafts. The most famous and distinctive is *nanduti* lace. Nanduti is the Guarani word for spiderweb, but the craft itself probably came to the New World from Spain. Nanduti lace's circular patterns depict themes such as animals and flowers.

During colonial times, Paraguayans developed their own artistic style in painting and wood carving. Art of this period used decorative Guarani themes. Pieces included religious paintings, murals, and figurines.

The **Maka people of Paraguay** are known for their weaving skill. This Maka woman is finishing a blanket woven with traditional methods and symbols.

In 1910 Pablo Alborno and Juan Samudio established the National Academy of Fine Arts in Asunción. Alborno had studied in Europe and introduced impressionism to Paraguay. He specialized in murals but also became well known for his landscapes and portraits. His best-known work is *Nanduti Lacemakers*, which depicts the traditional Paraguayan craft of making lace.

Another Paraguayan artist was Julián de la Herrería. He worked as a painter, etcher, and ceramist during the early 1900s. His art frequently showed indigenous Paraguayans. Around the same time, Jaime Bestard's paintings portrayed fiestas, processions, and landscapes.

During the mid-1900s, some Paraguayan art addressed the nation's rule by dictators. For example, Carlos Colombino, who painted on engraved wood, created many scenes of oppression and suffering under dictatorships.

More recent artists include Ricardo Migliorisi, who works as a painter as well as an architect and scenery designer. His work has won multiple international awards. Ofelia Olmedo's portraits are emotional and intense, while Félix Toranzos Miers is a painter, architect, and graphic designer who has won awards for his work.

Music and Dance

Like much of Paraguay's culture, its music shows Guarani influences. The sad tunes that featured in traditional Guarani music appear as themes in Paraguayan music. Some rural people still play indigenous instruments such as flutes made of sugarcane and rattles made of gourds. However, Spanish guitars and harps are more common in modern Paraguay.

MOVIE TIME

Local movie theaters in Paraguay show films from the United States and Europe as well as from South American nations. Paraguay also has a small but growing film industry of its own. The first film made in Paraguay was the ten-minute-long documentary *Alma Paraguaya*. Hipólito Carrón made this film in 1925. The nation's cinema suffered during Stroessner's rule, during which the arts and free speech were suppressed. Modern Paraguayan filmmakers are beginning to attract attention. One prominent recent movie was *Hamaca Paraguaya* (2006). It focuses on a rural Paraguayan family in 1935. This film was nominated for several awards and screened at international film festivals. Moviemakers from other countries have also used Paraguay as a setting. Part of the 2006 U.S. movie *Miami Vice* was filmed in Ciudad del Este, for instance.

Some of Paraguay's most popular music forms are the polka and the waltz—both of which have European origins. The Paraguayan polka (Danza Paraguaya) emerged in the 1800s. It gets its name from the European polka, which developed in Germany. But the Paraguayan polka—which has several versions—sounds very different, because it uses different rhythms.

Another typical form of local music is the Guarania. The composer José Asunción Flores created this style in 1925. It has a slow tempo and a melancholy character. The lyrics of Guarania songs often describe Paraguayan life or tell epic stories of national heroes.

More recently, several Paraguayan classical guitarists have gained international fame. Berta Rojas has performed around the world, and she has won many awards for her work. Fellow guitarist Luz María Bobadilla has also played concerts everywhere from Brazil to Israel, and she has a radio show back home in Paraguay.

Rock and popular music also have listeners in Paraguay. Bands performing these modern styles of music draw many large audiences to two music festivals in Asunción.

Many of the nation's traditional music forms are associated with dances. For example, during all fiesta (festival) times, people dance the Paraguayan polka late into the night. Older regional folk dances include the *danza de la botella* (bottle dance) in which performers balance flower-filled bottles on their heads.

A woman performs the bottle dance. In this traditional dance, a female dancer balances one or more bottles on her head while swaying to music. Other dancers circle around her.

▷ Food

The diet of most Paraguayans is quite simple. It features hearty and often starchy ingredients such as cassava and corn, as well as root vegetables such as yams and potatoes. Beans and peanuts also are featured in many dishes. Stews are common. One typical dish is *puchero*, made with meat (such as chicken or beef), vegetables, onions, and garlic.

The country's national dish is *sopa paraguaya*. Although its name means "Paraguayan soup," it is not soupy at all. It is a dense corn bread made with cheese, milk, and sometimes onions. Corn is also featured in *borí borí*, a soup made with balls of corn and cheese, as well as meat and vegetables. And cassava flour is the basis of *chipá*, a bread that also contains milk, eggs, and cheese. Cooks sometimes add corn to chipá as well.

While meat can be too expensive for everyday dining—especially among rural Paraguayans—beef is popular around the country. People often enjoy barbecued beef (asado) on Sundays. Pork is also popular and often appears on menus for special occasions. Paraguayans eat chicken and dine on fish such as the surubí, a huge catfish that swims the Paraná and other rivers.

WORLD'S BIGGEST BARBECUE

In 2008 Paraguay set a new world record. Cooks there prepared the world's biggest one-day barbecue, grilling more than 57,700 pounds (26,172 kg) of meat and serving more than thirty thousand people in about six hours. The money raised by the event was donated to charity to help children with cancer and women who are victims of domestic violence.

ASADO

Traditional asado is meat that is grilled outside. But this recipe can be prepared in the oven at any time of the year, no matter what climate you live in.

2 pounds steak, cut into strips

1 cup flour

1 teaspoon salt

½ teaspoon black pepper

3 tablespoons vegetable oil

1 small onion, diced

4 tomatoes, diced

2 green bell peppers, chopped

1 clove garlic, minced

2 cups water, hot

1. Preheat oven to 325°F (165°C).
2. Coat the steak with the flour. Sprinkle with salt and pepper.
3. Place oil in a frying pan, and heat over high heat. Add steak and brown on both sides (about 3 minutes per side).
4. Add remaining ingredients and sauté for about 5 minutes.
5. Transfer everything to a baking dish and cover with foil. Bake for about 2 hours or until tender.

Serves 6

The most popular beverage in Paraguay is a hot tealike drink called yerba maté. Men, women, and children sip maté out of hand-sized gourds through metal or wooden straws called *bombillas*. The drink contains a high level of caffeine. Paraguayans and many other South Americans drink it frequently throughout the day. A variety of rituals surround maté. For example, when people pass a bowl of maté around a group, it is considered rude to refuse a sip through the bombilla. Paraguayans also enjoy a cold version of maté called *tereré*.

A Guarani woman uses a bombilla to drink **maté tea.**

Paraguay's Julio César Cáceres *(right)* fights a Peruvian player for the ball during a 2008 soccer game in Asunción.

Sports and Recreation

As in most of South America, the most popular sport in Paraguay by far is *futbol* (soccer). People play it all across the country, at parks, fields, and formal clubs. Clubs usually have their own fields, and some have seating for as many as fifteen thousand spectators. Local teams compete internationally with others from South America and beyond. The country also has a national team, nicknamed the Guaranies and also called La Albirroja (White and Red). The team has competed in the World Cup, a tournament that brings together teams from all over the world every four years. Paraguay's national team also won the silver medal at the 2004 Summer Olympics in Athens, Greece.

Paraguay sent a team to the 2008 Summer Olympics in Beijing, China. Six athletes attended, competing in swimming, sailing, shooting, javelin throwing, and table tennis.

Visit www.vgsbooks.com for links to websites with additional information about Paraguay's culture. Listen to samples of Paraguayan music and get the latest news on Paraguay's athletes.

Basketball is another very popular sport in Paraguay. Paraguayans also enjoy volleyball, swimming, and tennis. Rossana de los Ríos is one of the nation's most famous tennis stars.

Other recreation in Paraguay includes hunting in the countryside and fishing in the nation's many rivers. People practice these hobbies as sport and also to obtain food. Horseback riding, a historical necessity for travel, has become a popular pastime in the capital and major towns.

THE ECONOMY

During the 1980s, Paraguay enjoyed one of the highest rates of economic growth in the Western Hemisphere. Much of this activity was a result of international aid for the construction of roads and hydroelectric projects.

By the mid-1990s, however, the country's economy was in decline. A worldwide recession (economic slowdown) lowered demand for Paraguayan goods. Increased competition from neighboring countries also harmed Paraguay business. And as exports slowed, the nation's foreign debt increased. Unemployment and prices rose sharply. In addition, the government was losing money through businesses that it owned and operated.

In the twenty-first century, Paraguay's leaders work to reform and improve the nation's economy. Steps in that direction have included selling many unprofitable public companies to private and foreign investors. The government has also borrowed money from international lending agencies. These loans help pay for further development, but

they also increase the nation's debt. Reducing debt and controlling infla-tion (rapidly rising costs of goods) still present challenges for Paraguay.

Services and Trade

Paraguay's service industry accounts for about 55 percent of its gross domestic product. (Abbreviated as GDP, gross domestic product is a measure of the total annual value of goods and services produced by a nation's workers.) Activities in the service sector include government work, banking, insurance, health care, retail sales, tourism, and other jobs that supply services rather then producing goods. This large sector also employs 52 percent of all the nation's workers.

Tourism is a major part of the nation's service sector and a valuable source of foreign income. Most visitors come from Argentina, Brazil, and other nations in the region. A smaller number arrive from the United States, Europe, and elsewhere. Many come to enjoy Paraguay's natural scenery and wildlife.

Foreign trade is another important aspect of Paraguay's economy. In 1991 Paraguay joined with Argentina, Brazil, and Uruguay to form the Mercado Común del Sur (Mercosur), a common trading market in southern South America. By joining Mercosur, these nations ended all trade barriers, including tariffs (taxes on trade items), among themselves in 1995. As a result, Paraguay trades largely with other Mercosur nations. Most of the country's exports go to Uruguay and Brazil. But Russia, the United States, and Switzerland are also important markets for Paraguayan goods. These exports include beef, soybeans, sugar, various types of seeds, and cereal grains. The country imports machinery, vehicles, chemicals, and mineral fuels. Most of these imports come from China, but many also come from Brazil and Argentina.

Agriculture

Agriculture was once the mainstay of Paraguay's economy. While it remains important, it has shrunk as an economic sector. Together with hunting, forestry, and fishing, agriculture makes up about 22 percent of Paraguay's GDP. It employs about 31 percent of the nation's workers.

In addition to helping feed Paraguay's own people, agriculture still accounts for most of the country's exports. Principal crops are cassava, soybeans, and sugarcane. Other agricultural products include corn, wheat, and a wide variety of fruits and vegetables.

Most rural families have plots of land where they raise their own food. Corn and cassava are staples, but people also grow sweet potatoes, onions, cabbages, peppers, lettuce, beans, and tomatoes. Among the fruits that thrive in the warm climate are grapes, citrus fruits, bananas, coconuts, pineapples, guavas (sweet, yellow fruits), mangoes, melons, and apricots.

Besides supporting fruits, vegetables, and grains, Paraguay's land is also suited for raising domestic animals. Dairy and beef cattle graze in the country's pastures. Paraguayans also raise chickens, sheep, pigs, ducks, and horses.

One challenge facing Paraguay's economy is that many of the nation's farms are too small to earn much money. Such small farms may produce enough to feed the families that work them. But they

SPECTACULAR SOY

Of all Paraguay's crops, soybeans have become the most valuable. Demand for this product has increased worldwide, especially in China. Meanwhile, soybean production in the United States has declined. Since the beginning of the 2000s, the amount of Paraguayan land devoted to soybean farming has increased almost five times.

Members of this **soybean farm cooperative in Paraguay** can share equipment like this pesticide sprayer.

are not big enough to compete with the larger and more modern farms of neighboring Brazil and Argentina. Most Paraguayan farmers cannot afford tractors, for example.

To help small farms compete, the Paraguayan government encourages agricultural cooperatives. Through cooperatives, farmers jointly purchase equipment that would be too expensive for an individual farmer to buy. Then they share the equipment. Cooperatives also help farmers save money on seeds, fertilizers, and other necessities.

Forestry is another valuable part of Paraguay's economy. The nation has huge areas of woodland with commercial potential. The government is trying to take advantage of this resource, while taking care to conserve forests and use them responsibly. Forest products include quebracho, holly tree leaves for yerba maté, citrus trees, rubber trees, and coconut plants.

Fishing is only a very small part of this landlocked country's economy. Rivers produce catfish, dorado, pacu, and other fish. But local people eat most of the catch, and the industry remains small.

Manufacturing and Industry

Manufacturing and industry comprise 23 percent of the country's GDP. They also employ 17 percent of its workers.

The principal manufactured products are food—including beef, sugar, and vegetable oils—and beverages such as soft drinks. Paraguay

A technician takes a sample at a **factory in Asunción.** The factory processes stevia plants, which produce a sweet liquid used in place of sugar.

also produces textiles, clothing, leather goods, chemicals, paper, cement, and wood products. Factories in the country include textile, flour, and paper mills.

Paraguay does not have a large mining sector. It does hold some mineral deposits, including marble, limestone, sandstone, and other resources. It also contains reserves of copper and manganese, plus a small amount of iron ore. But due to limited funds and difficult terrain, most of these resources have not been widely mined.

Transportation

Paraguay's road and highway system includes more than 9,300 miles (14,967 km) of paved roads. An additional 9,000 miles (14,484 km) of dirt roads crisscross the country. One of the largest and most important roads is the Pan-American Highway. Running from Asunción eastward to the Brazilian border, it carries an increasing volume of vehicles, including important commercial traffic. On the Brazilian side of the frontier, this paved route continues to Brazilian ports. It gives Paraguay a reliable, all-weather land route to transport its products to the outside world. The Pan-American Highway branches south toward Argentina as well. Regular bus service on the highway carries passengers to both Brazil and Argentina.

The **Friendship Bridge** spans the Paraná River at Ciudad del Este.

Another of Paraguay's major routes is the Trans-Chaco Highway. Running from Asunción to Bolivia, it cuts through the huge Chaco wilderness. This important addition to the country's transportation network has encouraged greater settlement in the Gran Chaco. But most of the country's commercially important roads are still located in the eastern and most populous regions.

Landlocked Paraguay has no ocean ports. But its rivers are important transportation routes. Asunción, situated on the Paraguay River, is the country's main port. Other ports are located at Villeta and San Antonio (on the Paraguay River), and Encarnación (on the Paraná).

More than a dozen international airlines service Silvio Pettirossi International Airport near Asunción. The busiest air routes from Asunción connect the capital to other major South American cities as well as to Madrid, Spain. Another international airport is located in Ciudad del Este, and smaller domestic airports are scattered around the country.

> Paraguay's Friendship Bridge crosses the Paraná River, linking Ciudad del Este and Foz do Iguaçu, Brazil. Most of Paraguay's imports and exports travel across this bridge.

Energy

Paraguay's energy production dates back to the 1960s, when Paraguay built huge hydroelectric dams along the Alto Paraná River. Constructed jointly with Brazilian funds, the Itaipú Dam and hydroelectric power plant produce huge amounts of energy. Argentine funds helped construct the Yacyretá hydroelectric power plant. Building these dams boosted Paraguay's economy by providing jobs for tens of thousands of workers. A whole range of related industries supplied the materials and equipment needed for dam construction. New towns created to house laborers and their families near the construction sites stimulated local agricultural efforts to feed the worker populations. By the late 1980s, the dams had doubled the value of Paraguay's total production of goods and services.

The Itaipú Dam, completed in 1981, is the world's second-largest source of hydroelectric energy, after China's Three Gorges Dam.

Hydroelectric dams continue to produce 99.9 percent of all electricity generated in Paraguay. Paraguay relies on this energy for its own needs. It is also a major exporter of power to nearby nations and one of the largest electricity producers in the world.

The construction of the Itaipú Dam created a huge lake called a reservoir.

Media and Communications

More than forty daily newspapers are published in Paraguay, helping keep residents up to date with news and other information. *ABC Color* and *La Nación* are among the papers with the most readers. A variety of radio stations broadcast music and news, as well as talk programs. Several television stations also broadcast in the country.

Many Paraguayans keep in touch by telephone. The nation has about 4.3 million cellular phones in use—approximately ten times the number of traditional landlines. In addition, Paraguay has more than 250,000 Internet users, a number that has grown rapidly since the beginning of the twenty-first century. Asunción residents have access to Internet cafés. Internet access is less common outside the capital.

Visit www.vgsbooks.com for links to websites with additional information about Paraguay's economy, including the most current information on imports and exports in Paraguay.

The Future

Alfredo Stroessner's fall in early 1989 brought about the end of dictatorship in Paraguay. During the early 1990s, Paraguayans hoped for a new, democratic era. But having brought dictatorship to a close, Paraguay next had to face serious economic problems, including inflation and unemployment.

Paraguay still faces challenges. But its leaders are working to continue strengthening the economy, as well as to provide the country's citizens with democracy, civil rights, and opportunity. If they succeed, the nation's future will be better and brighter for all of its people.

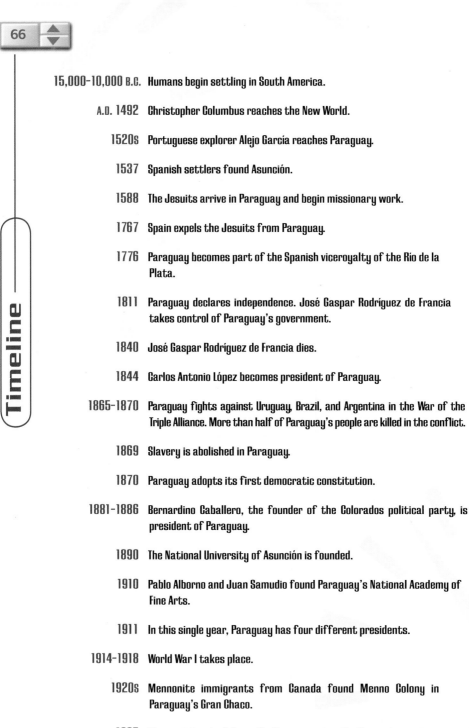

Timeline

15,000-10,000 B.C. Humans begin settling in South America.

A.D. 1492 Christopher Columbus reaches the New World.

1520s Portuguese explorer Alejo García reaches Paraguay.

1537 Spanish settlers found Asunción.

1588 The Jesuits arrive in Paraguay and begin missionary work.

1767 Spain expels the Jesuits from Paraguay.

1776 Paraguay becomes part of the Spanish viceroyalty of the Río de la Plata.

1811 Paraguay declares independence. José Gaspar Rodríguez de Francia takes control of Paraguay's government.

1840 José Gaspar Rodríguez de Francia dies.

1844 Carlos Antonio López becomes president of Paraguay.

1865-1870 Paraguay fights against Uruguay, Brazil, and Argentina in the War of the Triple Alliance. More than half of Paraguay's people are killed in the conflict.

1869 Slavery is abolished in Paraguay.

1870 Paraguay adopts its first democratic constitution.

1881-1886 Bernardino Caballero, the founder of the Colorados political party, is president of Paraguay.

1890 The National University of Asunción is founded.

1910 Pablo Alborno and Juan Samudio found Paraguay's National Academy of Fine Arts.

1911 In this single year, Paraguay has four different presidents.

1914-1918 World War I takes place.

1920s Mennonite immigrants from Canada found Menno Colony in Paraguay's Gran Chaco.

1925 The musician José Asunción Flores creates the Guarania musical style. Hipólito Carrón makes *Alma Paraguaya*, Paraguay's first locally made film.

1932-1935 Paraguay fights against Bolivia in the Chaco War.

1938 A formal treaty establishes the terms of peace after the Chaco War.

1939 World War II breaks out in Europe.

1940 President José Félix Estigarribia introduces a new
      constitution.

1944 Paraguay's president Higinio Morínigo declares war against the
      Axis powers in World War II. The war ends the following year.

1954 General Alfredo Stroessner becomes president. He rules as a dictator for
      more than thirty years. Under his regime, many Paraguayans are arrested,
      tortured, and murdered.

1969 Paraguay's men's basketball team wins the South American championship.

1981 Workers complete the Itaipú Dam. At the time, it is the largest hydroelectric dam
      in the world.

1989 A violent coup overthrows Stroessner. Andrés Rodriguez takes control of the
      government. Author Augusto Roa Bastos wins the Cervantes Prize for Literature.

1991 Paraguay and other South American nations form the trade organization Mercosur.

1992 The Archives of Terror—files detailing the fates of thousands of people arrested and
      killed in Paraguay under Stroessner's rule—are found.

1993 Juan Carlos Wasmosy wins Paraguay's first free and open presidential election.

1997 The System for the Vigilance of the Amazon (SIVAM) project begins collecting information
      to protect Paraguay's land and people from forest fires, floods, and pollution.

2000 An attempted coup to oust President Luis González Macchi fails.

2003 Protests break out demanding the redistribution of land.

2004 A fire in Asunción kills more than 420 people, and Paraguayans join in three days of
      national mourning. At the Summer Olympics in Athens, Greece, Paraguay's soccer team
      wins the silver medal.

2005 Paraguay hosts the world's first meeting of landlocked nations.

2008 Fernando Lugo becomes president, ending more than sixty years of political control
      by the Colorados.

2009 Juan Eduardo Samudio becomes Paraguay's all-time top scorer in soccer. Protests
      break out in Asunción over a high-ranking Stroessner official's return to
      Paraguay for medical care.

COUNTRY NAME Republic of Paraguay

AREA 157,048 square miles (406,752 sq. km)

MAIN LANDFORMS Gran Chaco, Paraná Plateau, Paraneña

HIGHEST POINT Cerro Pero, 2,762 feet (842 m) above sea level

LOWEST POINT junction of the Paraguay and Paraná rivers, 151 feet (46 m) above sea level

MAJOR RIVERS Acaray, Alto Paraná, Apa, Aquidaban, Iguazu, Jejui Guazú, Monte Lindo, Paraguay, Paraná, Pilcomayo, Tebicuary, Verde, and Ypané

ANIMALS anacondas, anteaters, bitterns, capybaras, jaguars, kingfishers, lungfish, ocelots, peccaries, piranhas, rheas, tapirs

CAPITAL CITY Asunción

OTHER MAJOR CITIES Ciuad del Este, Concepción, Encarnación, Villarrica

OFFICIAL LANGUAGES Spanish and Guarani

MONETARY UNIT guarani. 100 centimos = 1 guarani.

CURRENCY

Paraguay's national currency is the guarani. The country began issuing this currency in 1944. Guaranies are made up of 100 céntimos. However, because of inflation, these smaller units of currency are no longer in use. Bills come in values of 5,000, 10,000, 20,000, 50,000, and 100,000 guaranies. Some bills show cultural images such as a woman in traditional dress. Others have designs depicting famous people such as José Gaspar Rodríguez de Francia or Francisco Solano López, or historic events including the nation's declaration of independence. Paraguay also mints coins in denominations of 5, 10, 50, 100, 500, and 1,000 guaranies. Like banknotes, the coins feature images of historic figures and Paraguayan scenes.

Paraguay adopted its national flag in 1842. It is a tricolor style of flag, meaning that it has three stripes of different colors. The stripes are horizontal and are all the same width, with red on top, white in the middle, and blue on the bottom. On one side of the flag, in the middle of the white stripe, is the national coat of arms, a yellow star on a pale blue field. Intertwined branches of palm leaves and olive leaves form a wreath around the star. Above the seal are the words "Republica del Paraguay" (Republic of Paraguay). In the center of the flag's other side is the Seal of the Treasury, consisting of a lion and a Phrygian cap (a traditional symbol of liberty) on top of a pole. Above the lion is the national motto: "Paz y Justicia," meaning "Peace and Justice" in Spanish. Paraguay's flag is one of only a handful of national flags with different designs on the front and back.

Paraguay's national anthem is titled "Paraguayos, República o muerte!" (Paraguayans, republic or death!). The nation adopted the anthem in 1846, although the current version was not officially declared the country's anthem until 1934. Two Uruguayans actually wrote the anthem, with Francisco Esteban Acuña de Figueroa writing the anthem's words, and Francisco José Debali composing its music. The anthem's chorus follows below in both Spanish and English.

Paraguayos, República o muerte!
Nuestro brío nos dió libertad;
Ni opresores, ni siervos, alientan,
Donde reinan unión, e igualdad.

Paraguayans, Republic or death!
It was our strength that gave us our final liberty.
Neither tyrants nor slaves can continue,
Where unity and equality reign.

For a link to a site where you can listen to Paraguay's national anthem, "Paraguayos, República o muerte!" visit www.vgsbooks.com.

Note: Some Paraguayans' last names follow the Spanish style. The father's last name comes first, followed by the mother's last name. The father's last name is used in the shortened form and for alphabetization. For example, Félix Toranzos Miers takes the name Toranzos from his father, and Miers from his mother. In shortened form, he may be called Toranzos Miers or simply Toranzos.

MARTÍN ALMADA (b. 1937) Almada was born in Puertro Sastre, a town north of Concepción and close to Paraguay's border with Brazil. He studied education and also went on to earn a law degree. In the early 1970s, he became a vocal opponent of Alfredo Stroessner's regime, and in 1974, he was arrested as a political prisoner. During his imprisonment he was tortured. He was eventually released in 1977, due in part to the efforts of Amnesty International, a human rights organization. After regaining his freedom, Almada left Paraguay and wrote about his experiences as a political prisoner and torture victim. He later returned to his homeland, and in 1992, along with several other people, discovered the Archives of Terror.

AGUSTÍN BARRIOS MANGORÉ (1885–1944) Barrios was born in San Juan Bautista de las Misiones, in southern Paraguay. He was part of a large family, being the fifth child of seven, all of them boys. Barrios's family was very musical, and he began playing instruments himself at a young age. He grew up to be a composer and guitar player, and many people consider him one of Paraguay's greatest musicians. Barrios was a popular guitarist in concert, and he also recorded his playing on early records. He wrote both lyrics and music for his songs—more than three hundred of them—and often included themes from Paraguayan folklore.

FERNANDO LUGO (b. 1951) Lugo was born in San Solano, a small village in southeastern Paraguay. He was part of a politically active family, and his father hoped he would become a lawyer. Instead, he took a job as a teacher. Soon afterward, he developed a deep interest in religion and attended a seminary (a school that prepares people to become religious priests or other religious figures). At the age of twenty-six, he became a Catholic priest, and he later became a bishop. A bishop is a priest who is in charge of a diocese (a group of church administrative districts called parishes). But politics eventually entered Lugo's life. In the early 2000s, he decided to run for president. He stepped down from his position as bishop and ran for political office with promises to help Paraguay's poor. In April 2008, he was elected president.

SILVIO PETTIROSSI (1887–1916) Born in Asunción, Pettirossi had a passion for flying. The field of aviation was still young at the time. The American Wright brothers had only made their first successful, powered, piloted airplane flight in 1903. Eager to take part in this new field, Pettirossi went to Argentina to study with the pilot Jorge Newbery. In

1912 Pettirossi received a scholarship from Paraguay's government to continue his study of flight in France. He became well known in Europe and South America for his acrobatic flights. Pettirossi died when one of his plane's wings broke during an acrobatic trick, resulting in a crash. Asunción's international airport is named after him.

ROSSANA DE LOS RÍOS (b. 1975)

Ríos was born in Asunción. As a young girl, her talent and passion for tennis became clear. She played her first major tournament at the age of fourteen, in São Paulo, Brazil. She went on to play in many other matches in South America, and in 1992 she held the rank of the world's top junior tennis player. Since then she has continued to play around the world and is considered one of Paraguay's greatest athletes.

AUGUSTO ROA BASTOS (1917–2005)

Born in Asunción, Roa Bastos wrote his first play when he was thirteen years old. While he was still in his teens, the Chaco War broke out, and young Roa Bastos took part in the conflict. After the war's end, he returned to writing. He wrote for a newspaper and composed his own stories, plays, and poems. He was also involved in his country's politics. In 1947 he took part in the coup that brought Alfredo Stroessner to power. Roa Bastos and many others thought that Stroessner would be a good leader for Paraguay. But Stroessner proved to be more dictatorial than earlier leaders. To avoid being arrested by Stroessner's regime, Roa Bastos went into exile in Argentina. Much of his writing—especially his 1974 book, *Yo el Supremo (I, the Supreme)*—tackled social and political issues in Paraguay. He won the prestigious Cervantes Prize in 1989—the same year Stroessner lost power. Roa Bastos returned to Paraguay in 1996.

JUAN EDUARDO SAMUDIO (b. 1978)

Born in Asunción, Samudio is one of Paraguay's best-known soccer players. After playing on youth teams for a number of years, he went on to play professionally. While Samudio has played for several clubs, he has spent the most time on the Libertad team, based in Asunción. He is a striker, also known as a forward, and has participated in several South American tournaments. Samudio was the top goal scorer in Paraguay's top division of soccer teams in 2002 and 2004, and as of early 2009, he was Paraguay's all-time top scorer.

FÉLIX TORANZOS MIERS (b. 1962)

Toranzos Miers was born in Asunción. His father, Don Luis Toranzos, was an artist, and young Félix soon showed his own interest and talent in the visual arts. At first he focused on architecture but later began working on paintings and sculpture, as well as continuing to explore architecture. Exhibitions of his art have appeared in his native Paraguay as well as in other South American nations, and he has won several awards for his work. He also teaches art classes and workshops.

ASUNCIÓN As Paraguay's capital city and largest urban center, Asunción offers a variety of sights. One of its most impressive buildings is the Palacio de Gobierno, home of the country's president. Another noteworthy monument is the Pantheon of Heroes, which honors famous and heroic Paraguayans of the past. A number of attractive parks grace the city, including a botanical garden and a large cemetery. Asunción is also home to several museums such as the Museum of Natural History and a museum of indigenous history and culture.

THE GRAN CHACO The largely untouched wilderness of the Gran Chaco is a must-see for nature lovers. The region is rich in animals, birds, and plants—many of which are rare outside of Paraguay. A number of national parks and wildlife reserves protect these precious species. Mennonite communities also dot the Gran Chaco. Some—such as Filadelfia and Loma Plata—are home to small historical museums.

ITAIPÚ HYDROELECTRIC PROJECT Visitors with an interest in science and energy will want to see the huge Itaipú Dam. Located near Ciudad del Este, along Paraguay's border with Brazil, the dam is one of the world's most impressive engineering feats. Guided tours take visitors inside to see the dam's workings, including the massive machine room—which is more than half a mile (0.8 km) in length!

JESUIT MISSIONS After the Jesuits left Paraguay in 1767, their missionary centers fell into decay. Their ruins remain important architectural and historical monuments. The mission at Trinidad, about 17 miles (27 km) northeast of Encarnación, is one of the best-known Jesuit missions in Paraguay. Another grand restored church is at Jesús, a short distance north of Trinidad.

LAKE YPACARAÍ This lake is a popular resort area, and many charming villages and towns lie along its banks and in the surrounding region. For example, Itauguá, near the south side of the lake, is famous for nanduti lace. The town is also home to an art museum and a museum of indigenous history. Areguá, a settlement just west of the lake, is known for its ceramics. And the town of Ypacaraí, south of the lake, hosts an annual festival of music, dancing, poetry, and other arts.

CERRO CORÀ NATIONAL PARK This national park lies in central eastern Paraguay. It offers dramatic rock formations and broad plains, as well as wildlife including monkeys, tortoises, and armadillos. The park is also an important historical site. Ancient drawings decorate some of the park's rocks. And Paraguay suffered its defeat in the War of the Triple Alliance here in 1870. In this final battle, Francisco Solano López died at a site within the park's territory, and visitors can see monuments to him and other heroes of the war.

colony: a territory ruled and occupied by a foreign power

Communism: a political, social, and economic system based on the idea of common, rather than private, property. In a Communist system, the government controls land, resources, industry, and money and distributes them among its citizens.

coup: the forceful overthrow of or change in government by a small group. Some historic coups in Paraguay were carried out by members of the army and are called military coups.

deforestation: the widespread cutting down of forest lands

dictator: a leader who rules with complete control, often through the use of violence or other harsh methods

gross domestic product (GDP): a measure of the total value of goods and services produced within a country's boundaries in a certain amount of time (usually one year), regardless of the citizenship of the producers

hydroelectricity: electric power created by the force of rushing water

indigenous: native to a particular place

inflation: rapidly rising prices, usually paired with a decrease in the value of a nation's currency

junta: a ruling council, usually made up of a military or political group that has taken power by force. In Spanish, *junta* means "council" or "committee."

land reform: measures a government takes to redistribute farmland more equitably among its people

Latin America: Mexico, Central America, South America, and the islands of the West Indies. Latin America includes thirty-three independent countries, including Paraguay.

literacy: the ability to read and write a basic sentence. A country's literacy rate is one indicator of its level of human development.

Mennonites: members of an originally European religion who have settled in Paraguay and have formed their own communities, especially in the Gran Chaco

mestizo: a person of mixed European (usually Spanish) and indigenous ancestry. Most Paraguayans are mestizos.

missionary: a religious worker who works in a foreign country. Missionaries often attempt to convert people to Christianity, but they may also build hospitals, establish schools, and do other community work.

United Nations: an international organization formed at the end of World War II in 1945 to help handle global disputes. The United Nations replaced a similar, earlier group known as the League of Nations.

yerba maté: a tealike beverage made from the leaves of a South American shrub in the holly family. Yerba maté, often called simply "maté," is very popular in Paraguay and its neighboring countries.

Glossary

Box, Ben. *South American Handbook*. Bath, UK: Footprint, 2008.
This travel guide covers Paraguay and its fellow South American nations and includes historical, cultural, and geographical information.

Buckman, Robert T. *Latin America*. Washington, DC: Stryker-Post Publications, 2008.
Released yearly, this resource presents articles about the history and culture of Latin American nations.

Europa World Yearbook, 2008. Vol. 2. London: Europa Publications, 2008.
Covering Paraguay's recent history, economy, and government, this annual publication also provides a wealth of statistics on population, employment, trade, and more.

The International Year Book and Statesmen's Who's Who. London: Burke's Peerage, 2007.
An annually released reference material, this book provides information on Paraguay's economy, politics, people, and more.

Leuchars, Chris. *To the Bitter End: Paraguay and the War of the Triple Alliance*. Westport, CT: Greenwood Press, 2002.
A volume on military history, this book presents a history and analysis of the War of the Triple Alliance and Paraguay's role in it.

New York Times Company. *The New York Times on the Web*. 2008.
http://www.nytimes.com (December 10, 2008).
This online version of the newspaper offers current news stories along with an archive of articles on Paraguay.

Nickson, R. Andrew. *Historical Dictionary of Paraguay*. Metuchen, NJ: Scarecrow Press, 1993.
This reference book compiles information on everything from Paraguayan crafts to famous people.

"PRB 2008 World Population Data Sheet." *Population Reference Bureau (PRB)*. 2008.
http://www.prb.org (December 10, 2008).
This annual statistics sheet provides a wealth of data on Paraguay's population, birth and death rates, fertility rate, infant mortality rate, and other useful demographic information.

Turner, Barry, ed. *The Statesman's Yearbook: The Politics, Cultures, and Economies of the World, 2009*. New York: Macmillan Press, 2008.
This resource provides concise information on Paraguay's history, climate, government, economy, and culture, including relevant statistics.

UNDP. "Paraguay: 2007/2008 Report." *Human Development Reports*. 2008.
http://hdrstats.undp.org/countries/data_sheets/cty_ds_PRY.html (December 10, 2008).
The website, published by the United Nations Development Program (UNDP), presents a range of statistics on Paraguayan life. Information is available on health, education, the environment, and more.

Selected Bibliography

UNICEF. "At a Glance: Paraguay." *UNICEF: Information by Country*. 2008.
http://www.unicef.org/infobycountry/paraguay.html **(December 10, 2008).**
This site from the United Nations agency UNICEF offers details about education, nutrition, and other demographics in Paraguay.

U.S. Department of State. "Paraguay: Country Reports on Human Rights Practices—2007." *U.S. Department of State: Country Reports on Human Rights Practices*. 2008.
http://www.state.gov/g/drl/rls/hrrpt/2007/100649.htm **(December 10, 2008).**
This website is published by the U.S. State Department's Bureau of Democracy, Human Rights, and Labor. It provides a yearly update on the human rights situation within Paraguay, including concerns about women's rights, treatment of indigenous people, and other issues.

World Health Organization. "Paraguay." *World Health Organization: Countries*. 2008.
http://www.who.int/countries/pry/en/ **(December 10, 2008).**
This website provides a wealth of statistics and information on health issues in Paraguay.

BBC News—Americas
http://news.bbc.co.uk/2/hi/americas/default.stm
This news site provides a range of up-to-date information and archived articles about Paraguay and the surrounding region.

Capybara Facts
http://nationalzoo.si.edu/Animals/Amazonia/Facts/capybarafacts.cfm
This site from the National Zoo, in Washington, D.C., sets forth a few facts about capybaras—the largest rodents in the world, which are native to Paraguay.

CNN.com International
http://edition.cnn.com/WORLD/
Check CNN for current events and breaking news about Paraguay, as well as a searchable archive of older articles.

Draper, Allison Stark. *Hydropower of the Future: New Ways of Turning Water into Energy*. New York: Rosen Publishing Group, 2003.
Itaipú Dam produces most of Paraguay's energy though hydropower. This book examines this way of producing power.

Lonely Planet: Paraguay
http://www.lonelyplanet.com/paraguay
Visit this website for information about traveling to Paraguay. You can also learn some background information about the country at this site.

Paraguay: Sounds of Hope
http://www.pbs.org/frontlineworld/stories/paraguay604/
This site, associated with the PBS show *Frontline*, introduces Paraguayan music and musicians, as well as offering information about the country's history. View video, pictures, and more.

Parnell, Helga. *Cooking the South American Way*. Minneapolis: Twenty-First Century Books, 2003.
This cookbook presents a selection of recipes from Paraguay and its surrounding region. Cooks in Paraguay and throughout South America use many of the same ingredients and methods to prepare meals.

The Rough Guide to South America. New York: Rough Guides, 2004.
This travel guide to South America offers detailed information on visiting Paraguay, along with additional data on the country's culture and history.

Streissguth, Tom. *Argentina in Pictures*. Minneapolis: Twenty-First Century Books, 2003.
As Paraguay's neighbor to the southwest and as another former Spanish colony, Argentina shares many cultural and historical ties with Paraguay. Read this book to learn more about this nation.

Further Reading and Websites

————. *Brazil in Pictures*. Minneapolis: Twenty-First Century Books, 2003.

Like many other nations in South America, Brazil has historical, economic, and cultural ties to Paraguay. Learn more about Paraguay's northeastern neighbor in this book.

vgsbooks.com
http://www.vgsbooks.com

Visit vgsbooks.com, the home page of the Visual Geography Series®. You can get linked to all sorts of useful online information, including geographical, historical, demographic, cultural, and economic websites. The vgsbooks.com site is a great resource for late-breaking news and statistics.

Index

AIDS, 43
Almada, Martín, 70
animals, 15–16, 41, 72; capybara, 16
Archives of Terror, 35, 70
Argentina, 5, 8, 19, 23–24, 27, 30
arts and crafts, 51–52, 71, 72
asado (barbecue), 54, 55
Asunción, 9, 18–19, 21–22, 38, 43, 45, 49, 72, 80

Barrios Mangoré, Agustín, 70
Bolivia, 8, 29–30
bottle dance, 53
Brazil, 5, 8, 27, 38, 62

capybara, 16
Carnival, 80
censorship, 52
Chaco War, 29–31, 71
cities, 18–19; Asunción, 9, 18–19, 21–22, 38, 43, 45, 49, 72, 80; Ciudad del Este, 19; Concepción, 19; Encarnación, 9, 19, 23; Villarrica, 19
civil and human rights, 5, 34, 35, 36, 37, 43, 65, 70
clothing, 40, 41
Cold War, 34
Colorados, 28, 32, 34, 35, 36
Communism, 34

deforestation, 17
dictatorships, 5, 24–26, 31–34, 65

economy, 7, 19, 42, 43, 58–65; agriculture, 40–41, 60–61; communications, 65; energy, 4, 11, 17, 64; industry and manufacturing, 61–62; loans, 32; mining, 17, 62; services, 59–60; tourism, 59; trade, 19, 60, 63; transportation, 62–63
education, 44–45
environmental issues, 17–18
Estigarribia, José Félix, 31
ethnic groups, 29, 39; arts of, 51, 52; Guarani, 4, 7, 13, 20, 22–23, 36, 37, 39, 46, 50–51; Maka, 51, 80

family life, 42–43

farms and farming, 12, 16, 18, 29, 40–41, 80
Festival of Alfalfa, 48
food, 54–55, 60; recipe, 55
forestry, 61
Francia, José Gaspar Rodríguez de, 24–25
Friendship Bridge, 63

Gran Chaco, 8, 9, 11, 13, 14, 63, 72; war over, 29–31
gross domestic product (GDP), 59, 60, 61
Guarani, 4, 7, 39, 46; in history, 20, 22–23; land reform and, 36, 37; language, 4, 7, 13, 23, 50; literature and, 50–51

health, 16, 36, 43–44
history, 4–5, 7; ancient, 4, 20, Chaco War, 29–31, 71; democracy, 7, 35–37, 65; dictatorships, 5, 24–26, 31–34, 65; independence, 5, 24–25; Jesuit missions, 22–23, 72; revolutions, 28, 32; Spanish rule, 4–5, 18, 21–24, 50; Stroessner's regime, 5, 33–34, 35, 65, 70, 71; War of the Triple Alliance, 5, 27, 28, 30
holidays and festivals, 48–49, 53, 80
housing, 40, 41
human trafficking, 43
hydroelectricity, 4, 11, 17, 33, 64, 72

Iguazu Falls, 12
Internet, 65
Itaipú Dam, 17, 19, 33, 64, 72

Jesuit missions, 22–23, 46, 72

lace making, 51–52
Lake Ypacaraí, 13, 72
land reform, 36
languages, 4, 7, 13, 50; Guarani, 13, 23, 50; official, 51; names, 13, 70
Latin America, 7, 34, 35
life expectancy, 43
lifestyles: rural, 12, 36, 41, 42, 43, 45, 60; urban, 18–19, 38, 40–41
literacy, 44

literature, 50–51, 71
López, Carlos Antonio, 25–26
López, Francisco Solano, 5, 26–27, 72
Lugo, Fernando, 37, 70

maps, 6, 10
Mbywangi, Margarita, 37
media, 65
Morínigo, Higinio, 31–32
mountains and hills, 8, 9
movies, 52
music and dance, 52–53, 70, 80

names, 13, 70
nanduti lace, 51–52
national parks, 13, 18, 72
natural resources, 4, 17–18

Pan-American Highway, 62
Paraguay: boundaries, size, and
   location, 4, 8; climate, 11, 14–15;
   currency, 68; flag, 69; flora and
   fauna, 14–16; government, 37;
   maps, 6, 10; national anthem, 69;
   population, 38; topography, 8–13
petroleum, 17, 30
Pettirossi, Silvio, 70–71
political parties, 28, 34
pollution, 17–18
population, 38
poverty, 7, 24, 36, 37, 38, 40, 43
Presidential Palace, 80

railways, 19
rainfall, 15
recipe, 55
regions, 8–9, 11
religions, 46–48; Christianity, 22,
   46–49, 70, 80; Mennonites, 46–47;
   traditional, 20, 47
Ríos, Rossana de los, 71
rivers, 4, 9, 11–13, 16, 80; dams on,
   64. *See also* hydroelectricity
Roa Bastos, Augusto, 50, 71
roads, 11, 33, 62–63
rodeos, 49
Rodríguez, Andrés, 5, 34, 35
rural life, 12, 36, 41, 42, 43, 45, 60

Samudio, Juan Eduardo, 71

sanitation, 40
slavery, 22–23, 39
Soviet Union, 34
soybeans, 60, 61
Spanish rule, 4–5, 18, 21–24, 50
sports and recreation, 56–57, 71
Stroessner Matiauda, Alfredo, 5,
   33–34, 35, 52, 65, 70
Supremo Dictador, El (the Supreme
   Dictator), 24

television, 65
Toranzos Miers, Félix, 71
torture, 35, 70
tourism, 59
transportation, 11, 19, 41, 62–63

United Nations, 32
United States, 29, 30, 32, 33–34
urban population, 18, 19, 38
Uruguay, 5, 27

War of the Triple Alliance, 5, 27, 28,
   30
water, 12, 43
Weaving, 51
women, 37, 42
World War II, 32, 39

yerba maté, 55

Captions for photos appearing on cover and chapter openers:

Cover: Women perform a traditional dance during a Carnival parade in Paraguay. Carnival is an early spring holiday that happens several weeks before Easter.

pp. 4–5 The Presidential Palace overlooks the Paraguay River in Asunción.

pp. 8–9 The Paraná River flows through some of Paraguay's most heavily populated areas.

pp. 38–39 Members of the Maka ethnic group perform a traditional dance during Paraguay's Indigenous Day celebration in Asunción.

pp. 46–47 Catholics visit the Basilica of Caacupé during a religious festival in the Paraguayan town of Caacupé.

pp. 58–59 A farmer sprays pesticides across a field of soybeans in western Paraguay.

Photo Acknowledgments

The images in this book are used with the permission of: © Photononstop/ SuperStock, pp. 4-5, 46-47; © XNR Productions, pp. 6, 10; © Martin Barlow/ Art Directors & TRIP, pp. 8-9; © André Chang/Travel-Images.com, pp. 11, 12, 16, 51; © Bobby Haas/National Geographic/Getty Images, p. 13; © Norberto Duarte/AFP/Getty Images, pp. 14, 36, 44, 48, 49; © Tom Brakefield/Stockbyte/ Getty Images, p. 15; © age fotostock/SuperStock, p. 17; © De Agostini Picture Library/Getty Images, p. 18; © Photo12/The Image Works, p. 22; © Kevin Moloney/Aurora/Getty Images, p. 23; © Mary Evans Picture Library/The Image Works, pp. 25, 27; © Hulton Archive/Getty Images, p. 26; © Samba Photo/ LatinContinent/Getty Images, p. 29; © Bettmann/CORBIS, pp. 30, 31; © Frank Scherschel/Time & Life Pictures/Getty Images, p. 33; AP Photo/Jorge Saenz, pp. 38-39, 56; © Christopher Pillitz/Reportage/Getty Images, p. 40; © Heiner Heine/Imagebroker/FLPA, pp. 41, 58-59, 61; © Imagebroker/Alamy, pp. 42, 45, 55; © COVER/The Image Works, p. 50; © O. Louis Mazzatenta/National Geographic/Getty Images, p. 53; © Jorge Romero/AFP/Getty Images, p. 54; © Daniel Caselli/AFP/Getty Images, p. 62; © Christopher Pillitz/The Image Bank/Getty Images, p. 63; © SambaPhoto/Cassio Vasconcellos/LatinContinent/ Getty Images, p. 64; Image courtesy of Banknotes.com – Audrius Tomonis, p. 68; © Laura Westlund/Independent Picture Service, p. 69.

Front cover: © Simon Hathaway/Alamy. Back cover: NASA.